W9-CYW-882

Anchors
of Hope

Volume Two

Anchors of Hope

Words of Life for the Soul

Volume Two

Hal M. Helms

PARACLETE PRESS
Brewster, Massachusetts

Unless otherwise designated, Scripture quotations are taken from the
Revised Standard Version of the Bible, copyright 1946, 1952, 1971 by
the Division of Christian Education of the National Council of the
Churches of Christ in the USA. Used by permission.

Scripture quotations designated (NIV) are taken from the Holy Bible,
New International Version®. NIV®. Copyright © 1973, 1978, 1984 by
International Bible Society. Used by permission of Zondervan Publishing
House. All rights reserved.

Library of Congress Cataloging-in-Publication Data

    Helms, Hal McElwaine.
    Anchors of Hope/Hal M. Helms.
    p.cm.
    Contents: v. 1. Words of life for the soul.
    ISBN 1-55725-172-X
    1. Aged—Prayer-books and devotions—English.
    2. Aging—Religious aspects—Christianity—
        Meditations. 3. Devotional calendars.
    I.Title.
    BV4580.H33   1996
    242'.65—dc20   96-34156
                          CIP

10 9 8 7 6 5 4 3 2 1

© 1997 by The Community of Jesus, Inc.
ISBN #: 1-55725-179-7

All rights reserved.

Published by Paraclete Press
Brewster, Massachusetts
Printed in the United States of America.

Cover photo credit:
photo # V76L 256030-2P; Tony Stone Images

Table of Contents

Foreword

"In hope that sends a shining ray far down the future's broadening way."

These words of Washington Gladden have been a favorite of mine for many years. Instead of seeing life becoming darker, more ominous and negative, he pictured a gleam of light shining on our pathway. That is what Jesus promised when he said to his disciples, and through them to all of us, "Lo, I am with you always, to the close of the age" (Matthew 28:20).

In this book, with readings for the second half of the year, we continue to look at life in this way. To be sure, life is difficult. At times it is very difficult indeed. We face uncertainties of many kinds. We suffer bodily aches and growing weakness as we grow older. We live in a world which has many negative features. At times, we may draw near to the edge of the grave. What do we carry with us in this journey? The light of hope. The sure promise of God's presence. Grace sufficient for every situation and every need. That is the solid foundation of the path on which we travel.

But we need to be reminded of all this. Second Peter 1:12 says, "So I will always remind you of these things, even though you know them and are firmly established in the truth you now have" (NIV). When difficulties arise, we need to be armed to claim the hope set before us. Our hope is not only for the presence of God as we journey. It goes far beyond that, and bids us look up to another country, the true Promised Land of which our fathers and mothers sang. Hope leads us onward.

Hope. Hope for the best. Look for the best. Look for God's love every day. Let the words of this little book encourage you to *look up*, and see God's merciful hand guiding you and strengthening you to carry on.

> "In hope that sends a shining ray far down the future's
> broadening way,
> In peace that only thou canst give, with thee, O Master,
> let me live."

Hal M. Helms

Secure in Him

Therefore I tell you, do not worry about your life, what you will eat or drink; or about your body, what you will wear. Is not life more important than clothes? Look at the birds of the air; they do not sow or reap or store away in barns, and yet your heavenly Father feeds them. Are you not much more valuable than they? . . .

MATTHEW 6:25-26 (NIV)

Taps

I will always see you
straight and tall
against the setting sun,
your customary khakis
replaced by civilian clothes.

You and I are
headed home from
the post dispensary—
an eight-year-old's
ear-ache emergency.
As the sun dips
below the horizon,
taps sounds
through the sultry
mid-summer haze
while the flag is lowered.

You pull over to
the side of the road
and turn off the ignition.
You get out,
and stand facing the flag
hand over your heart.

I join you
until the final note
dies away,
then in silence
we return
to the car
and continue our way home.

In that brief moment
forty years ago
you shared with me
something
of yourself,
and gave me
something
to believe in.

Sister Catherine

But Jesus Came

Revelation 1:4-8 and John 20:19-31

The doors were shut, but Jesus came and stood among them,
and said, "Peace be with you." JOHN 20:26B

One week after Easter, the disciples were still trying to grasp what it all meant. Reports were still being shared about the appearances of Jesus, and it was just too good to believe. It was a dangerous time, and the disciples were huddling together, "keeping a low profile," as we would say today. So when they gathered, they had the doors "shut for fear of the Jews." They did not know when that awful knock at the door might come which could lead them to the cross.

We need to stop and think a moment about what it was like. There are two things at work here: fear and foreboding about their own situation, and a recurring assurance from Jesus that he is alive and has overcome their real enemy—Satan and death. So they are like us in so many ways. We live in that kind of dichotomy between faith and fear. As you read this, you may know exactly what I'm talking about in your own case—your fears, your concerns about yourself or those you love, your health problems or even financial worries, your feelings of frustration that your life is more confined or less rewarding that it used to be. Whatever it is for us, the problems threaten to take away our joy and eagerness for life itself.

In our preoccupation with ourselves, we, too, may have shut the door of our life, shut ourselves in, so to speak. But then we can turn to our text: "The doors were shut, but Jesus came and stood among them." Even the shut doors could not keep him out! And that is truly wonderful, because in spite of all we may have done to close ourselves in, he has come to us, and stands ready to say the same thing to us he said to his friends then: "Peace be with you."

The Spirit Gives Life   JULY 2

Psalm 103 and II Corinthians 3:1-6

For the written code kills, but the Spirit gives life.
II CORINTHIANS 3:6

Paul is talking, of course, about the Old Covenant which God made with the people of Israel under Moses when the Law was given to them. It was a Covenant in which God promised to be the savior and deliverer of the people of Israel if they would remain faithful and obedient to him. Of course, the sad story is they did not, and they suffered defeat and disaster.

Now, Paul is saying, since Jesus came, a new Covenant has been established with the new Israel, the people of God—all those who would come to God through faith in his Son Jesus Christ, Jew and Gentile alike. This new Covenant was ratified in his blood on the Cross and sealed by the Holy Spirit. What does that mean? In our relationship with God, we are not to be lured into spiritual pride because of the good things we do, or because of what we do not do. If we are God's children, it is natural that we should try to please him, honor him, and show forth his glory to others. But we must be careful not to think that we are better than we are, and remember that it is the mercy and grace of God which is the foundation of our faith.

The letter kills. Whenever we begin to chalk up virtues for ourselves, we kill something inside us. We kill that tender, delicate part that is sensitive to others, quickly willing to see when we are wrong, open to the gentle moving of the Holy Spirit. We should so treasure and value this tender part of our heart that we beware of the temptation to think too highly of ourselves. The Spirit gives life. Abundant, flowing life, like a running brook, springs in the desert, dry moments of life that spring forth unexpectedly! Don't get hung up on winning arguments, having the right opinions, always doing the right thing, justifying yourself if you make a mistake. Just let the Spirit give you life more and more day by day.

What Is God Like? JULY 3

I Peter 2:2-10 and John 14:1-14

He who has seen me has seen the Father. . . . Believe me that I am in the Father and the Father in me, or else believe me for the sake of the works themselves. JOHN 14:9B AND 11

Psalm 76 says, "In Judah God is known" (Psalm 76:1). We did not make him up or invent a picture of who he is. We know him because he has made himself known.

There is always a temptation to make God like ourselves, to imagine that he thinks and feels as we do. It is a shock when we realize that his thoughts and ours are very, very different. He tells us that through the Bible: "My thoughts are not like your thoughts," says the Lord. "For as the heavens are high above the earth, so are my thoughts higher than your thoughts" (Isaiah 55:8,9). If we would truly know God, the real God, then we need to learn what he has revealed to us about himself.

Here is where we find this word of Jesus so helpful. After all the revelation of God we find in the Old Testament, Jesus comes to reveal, in a way that we can understand, what God is like. When we learn what Jesus is like, we know what the Father is like. I find that very reassuring, and a real comfort when I am facing some difficult point in my life. I cannot say that I have allowed it to remove all fear and anxiety, for sometimes I still have to struggle with feelings of aloneness and isolation. But then I look at Jesus—reaching out to help the helpless, befriending those who had no claim on him except his love and care for them. And then I find new inspiration for hope and a way out of the burden of fear.

Acquaint yourself with Jesus. Learn what the Bible tells you about him, and learn to listen to his voice within your heart. Talk with him as with a friend, and let him reassure you that he loves you, and that the Father loves you as well. "He who has seen me has seen the Father." That is what God is like.

Sweet Land of Liberty   JULY 4

Deuteronomy 15:7-11 and Galatians 5:1, 13-23

Blessed is the nation whose God is the Lord.   PSALM 33:12

Is there anywhere in the world where true freedom is enjoyed—except in those places where worship of God is guaranteed by law, and where his Word is preached, taught and obeyed? I think not.

But having rights given us by law does not guarantee that we will be free. We can have many legal rights and be slaves inside ourselves. Many Americans today are slaves to drugs, alcohol, sex, violence, anger, fear, lust for money or power. And no government or institution can make us free inside. That has to come from somewhere else. But how grateful we should be to live in a land where the gospel of Jesus Christ, the truth that sets us free, can be freely preached and practiced without fear of our being thrown into jail. How grateful we should be that as individuals we have been entrusted with that truth. We have heard with our ears the good news that can make us free people, whether we are physically free or limited by bodily ailments or other circumstances. The truth of Jesus can make all the difference. Jesus said, "If the Son makes you free, you will be free indeed." And that's the freedom God wills for you.

Helen Keller was blind and deaf from infancy. But her life showed that she was inwardly free—through her faith in God and his gift of determination to press through every difficulty. Beethoven, deaf in his outward hearing, could nonetheless compose the Ninth Symphony because he heard the music of the spheres! You and I, whatever limitations we have to face, can be free in heart and spirit if we choose to put our trust in Jesus Christ and live in his presence daily. Our very limitations can be a wonderful opportunity to explore our "inner space," something we might never have done without them.

Yes, thank God for this "sweet land of liberty." And even more, thank him for the truth that sets us free.

Life that is Life Indeed   JULY 5

I Timothy 6:6-19 and Luke 16:19-31

*. . . So that they may take hold of the life
which is life indeed.* I TIM. 6:19B

Today's Scriptures talk about false riches and true riches. And most of us need to hear these truths again and again, for it is so easy to mistake the false ones for the true ones.

Jesus cautions us, in this parable of the rich man who

died and went to the place of torment, that we can make some very serious mistakes by making wrong choices. That's what this man had done. He had lived for the wrong thing. He did not care about other people, but thought primarily of his own happiness and well-being.

Paul, writing from the Roman prison where he would later be put to death, tells Timothy to remind people that "There is great gain in godliness with contentment" (I Timothy 6:6). So learning to be content with our lot has some very important consequences—both for this life and for the life to come. This is true, because even in the next life, we will be what we have been becoming in this one. We take with us when we die what we are, who we are, what we have become!

As so he gives us this word of caution: Tell them, he says, to be rich in good deeds, liberal and generous, "so they may take hold of the life that is life indeed." That is the abundant life Jesus came to give us all. He did not promise us riches, fame, fortune, worldly glory. But he did say we could have the peace that passes understanding, deep and abiding in our hearts, even in trouble and times of uncertainty. That is the life Paul is talking about, and that is the life we should claim by faith every day.

He Looks for You   JULY 6

Psalm 32 and Luke 19:1-10

For the Son of man came to seek
and save the lost.   LUKE 19:10

This story of Zacchaeus, the short tax-collector, has always been a favorite. Zacchaeus was not a popular figure. He belonged to a hated class of people who collected taxes from the Jews for the Roman overlords. Scholars tell us that this was a kind of private enterprise, and the tax collectors could collect as much as possible, then pay the Romans a certain amount and keep the rest. It was apparently a lucrative business, but their fellow Jews hated them and considered them near-traitors.

Zacchaeus was hungry. He was hungry inside for something money could not buy. There was an emptiness there that he had never been able to fill. And when he heard these wonderful stories about Jesus, that hunger became even greater. It was so great that he climbed up in a tree to catch a glimpse of Jesus as he passed by. Can you imagine how he felt when Jesus stopped, called him by name, and invited himself to Zacchaeus's home?

"The Son of man came to seek and save the lost." Zacchaeus was lost. But after Jesus entered his home and his life, things were different. He had found a new meaning to his life. Money no longer held first place. "Half my goods I give to feed the poor." There was something in that relationship with Jesus that was more precious than gold.

It is still true today. Everything we long for, everything that makes life worth living, is hidden in our faith in Jesus Christ. His mercy and his goodness support us and give us hope. On our part, we are to welcome him. Open the door of your heart to believe in him and trust his goodness. He will not fail you. He cannot fail you, because he is faithful. When you feel lost, bewildered, confused or discouraged, that's a good time to say, "Lord, come into my heart. I need You and I welcome You. Come into my heart, Lord Jesus."

That I May Know Him JULY 7

Isaiah 43:16-21 and Philippians 3:8-14

I count everything as loss . . . that I may gain Christ and be found in him. . . , that I may know him and the power of his resurrection. PHILIPPIANS 3:8A AND C, 10A

When we first read these words of the great Apostle, we may wonder why he would write such things. After all, he, more than any of the other apostles, gave himself without reservation to take the gospel to the whole world. And in his labors, he wrote a great part of what we now call the New Testament. His writings set forth in the clearest possible way what it means to trust in Jesus Christ for this life and for the next. Every generation since his time has been indebted to him for his faithful work.

Yet here, writing to that little group of Christians in Philippi from his Roman prison, Paul gives us an insight into what makes him tick, so to speak. He has suffered a great deal as a Christian. At almost any time, if he had chosen, he could have spared himself the persecution and hardships he underwent if he had been willing to compromise his faith or go back on it.

In this passage he reviews his "credentials" as a God-fearing, law-abiding Jew. His pedigree was perfect. *But*, he says, "I count everything as loss because of the surpassing worth of knowing Christ Jesus my Lord." There are some things worth everything. Some things are worth giving your life for. If not, you will just fritter your life away and come to nothing.

But Paul knows the secret! Into that swift-flowing stream of life, he has found a Savior, a Lord, a Very Present Help— Jesus Christ. But oh, the thrill, the wonder, the joy of being loved, being sought and found, being lifted up to new hope! That is what Paul already had, and what we already have, if we just rest in Christ, who he is, what he has done for us, and what he is doing today. What is everything else in comparison? For it all slips away, whether we like it or not, and only that which is from God and of God remains. So let us rejoice today in him and seek to know him more fully as the hours slip by.

One Thing You Lack   July 8

Hebrews 4:1-3, 9-13 and Mark 10:17-30

And Jesus looking upon him, loved him and said to him, "One thing you lack, go, sell everything you have, and give to the poor, and you will have treasure in heaven. Then come, follow me."
Mark 10:21

This Gospel story is one of the most fascinating incidents in the life of Jesus. It describes a man who wanted to find peace and fulfillment in his life. He was a well-to-do or rich man. We call him "the Rich Young Ruler," but the point is not his age, but the lack of satisfaction he had in his life. Jesus says, like any good Jewish teacher, "you know the commandments," and names some of them. "I've kept them all," replies the man (probably a little self-righteously!). Then comes the startling point in the story: "You lack one thing. . . ."

And that's all it took. Jesus put his finger on the very place where the man was not willing to submit his heart and life to God. Because of that one thing, he could not find the life and peace his heart craved and longed for. With the "rich ruler" (young or old), it was his great possessions. Possessions are no blessing when they possess us. But it's not only giving up material things that Jesus is talking about here. It is whatever we hold back that keeps us from giving ourselves to God. He will not require it of us, and if we choose, we can walk away sorrowful, like the man in this story. But remember that Jesus "looking upon him loved him." How disappointed Jesus must have been that the man chose his tawdry things, whatever he was holding back, and missed the abundant life he wanted to share with him.

Counting the Cost   JULY 9

Philemon 1-20 and Luke 14:25-33

For which of you, desiring to build a tower, does not first sit down and count the cost, whether he has enough to complete it?   LUKE 14:28

I suppose few of us have any idea what it is going to mean when we decide to follow Jesus. We may have our heads full of romantic notions that everything is going to be wonderful. But if we had such ideas it is because we did not read and heed this passage from our Lord's own words!

This section of Luke's Gospel is surely one of the hardest sayings of Jesus—so hard that most Christians choose to ignore much of it, or convince themselves he didn't really mean what he seems to be saying. He talks about hating father, mother, wife, children, brothers, sisters, and even one's own life, saying that unless we do, we cannot be his disciples. Of course we have to balance that with his other words that bid us to love one another as he loved us and the strong word that if we hate our brother we do not know him. Neither of these is an easy word. It is hard to know just what it means to "hate" those we love, and it is sometimes hard to love them as he loved us. So we are caught in the middle!

Quite simply, I think Jesus is again warning us not to let any affection, any attachment, come between us and our heavenly Father. When Jesus says we should count the cost, he is telling us that there will be costs involved if we want to belong to him. I don't know what that means for you, but I know that he will show you in your daily life. He will show you and invite you to keep on taking up your cross, which he is always willing to help you bear. He never asks us to bear our cross alone!

On the Emmaus Road   JULY 10

Psalm 116:12-19 and Luke 24:13-35

Then they told what had happened on the road, and how he was known to them in the breaking of the bread.
LUKE 24:35

Surely this story of the Emmaus Road is a favorite of all of us. First, the disciples did not expect Jesus to go with them on the road. They were sad, grief-filled, preoccupied with their own feelings. And what about us? Are we not more likely simply to live our days with little or no expectation that he will really be with us? I think the reason for that, more than anything else, is that we have gotten into the habit of not expecting him. Let us learn to expect Jesus to accompany us on the road!

As they talked with Jesus (not knowing yet who he was) they had an inner sense that something wonderful was happening. "Did not our hearts burn within us while he talked to us on the road, while he opened the Scriptures?" (Luke 24:32). Have you ever had the experience of reading the Bible and found it speaking strongly, powerfully, tenderly to your heart, as though it was meant just for you and your need? We all should have that experience over and over again. We can have it if we read it believing that God will speak to us in that special way. Our hearts, too, can burn within us as he talks to us, opening the Scripture to our minds and hearts.

Third, it was in the breaking of the bread that Jesus was fully recognized by those disciples on the first Easter. And as soon as they knew him, it was enough. Earlier, they had said, "Abide with us, for it is evening, and the day is far spent." But now, knowing him, fed by his hand, they were eager to hurry back to share the good news with the others.

We have our Emmaus Road—when we do not sense how near he is. Yet he walks with us, and at our invitation, does indeed abide with us. Even more, he feeds us with his own strength so that we can live for others and not be absorbed in our own needs and cares. May you find him on your Emmaus Road!

Peace, Be Still!   JULY 11

II Corinthians 5:16-21 and Mark 4:35-41

*And he awoke and rebuked the wind, and said to the sea,
"Peace, be still!" And the wind ceased, and there was a
great calm.*   MARK 4:39

Those disciples with Jesus in the boat wanted enough wind to carry them smoothly along. But when the wind got too strong, they cried out, "Lord, do you not care if we perish?" There are many, many things in life that evade any easy, surface explanation. And if we angrily demand of God that he give us an explanation of why the sea of our life is so rough, it may seem indeed as though he has gone to sleep. God does not explain why things are the way they are. What we need is not explanation, but help when the sea of life gets too rough, when life gets too difficult.

What did Jesus do when they woke him up with their prayers? He rebuked the wind. He spoke to the situation. The wind was never out of his control. It only seemed to be. God is always in charge. And when the time was right, Jesus spoke the effective word, "and the wind ceased."

No matter what the trouble, no matter what the situation or difficulty we may be facing today, in God's time, in answer to our earnest prayer, he will rebuke the wind and it will cease. Many problems and heartaches may actually be something we have helped to cause. The disciples' decision had placed them on the sea at that moment. That was something they had done. Many of our problems are related to things we have done badly or mistakenly, or with wrong motives. God knows that, and allows the storm to clear the air. It brings our awareness that we are not God and not able to control life as we would like. And knowing that, we can see places where we have been wrong. Then we can say, "I am sorry I did this or that, or felt this way or that." Storms do accomplish something that fair weather cannot achieve.

And when the storm has done its work, whatever it is in us, Jesus himself will say, "Peace! be still!" He did it then and he will do it for us now.

Another Look at Prayer   JULY 12

Isaiah 50:4-9 and Mark 9:14-29

And he [Jesus] said to them, "This kind cannot be driven out by anything but prayer."   MARK 9:29

The incident of the father with the demon-possessed son was a difficult "learning experience" for the disciples. While Jesus, Peter, James and John were on the Mount of Transfiguration (in the beginning of Mark chapter 9), the other disciples faced the desperate request of this father for help with his son. When they failed, and Jesus returned, the man said simply, "I asked your disciples to cast it out, and they were not able" (Mark 9:18).

As we read the rest of the story, there are many things we should notice. Jesus' immortal words: "All things are possible to him who believes!" What a breath-taking thought! What an invitation to greater, more daring faith! What a scary possibility! And the father's response (some manuscripts of the Gospel add that he spoke "with tears"): "Lord I believe, help my unbelief!" His belief was only partial. It was strong enough to have prompted him to bring his son. But there was still "unbelief," and he needed help to overcome it. Then Jesus answered his prayer with that authoritative word: "Come out of him and never enter him again!"

Then, in answer to the question of the disciples, "Why could we not cast it out?" Jesus said, "This kind cannot be driven out by anything but by prayer." Again, some ancient manuscripts add the words "and fasting." That suggests to me that there are some problems in life that require persistent, earnest, unceasing prayer. They are the hard cases in our lives that don't yield to a quick fix.

That's where persistent prayer comes in. We have to ask and keep on asking; seek and keep on seeking; knock and keep on knocking—knowing that sooner or later, if we are faithful, the answer will come!

Persistent Prayer and Delayed Answers   July 13

Exodus 16:2-4, 9-16 and Matthew 15:21-28

But she [the Canaanite woman] came and knelt before him and said, "Lord, help me." . . . Then Jesus answered her, "O woman, great is your faith! Be it done for you as you desire."
MATTHEW 15:25 AND 28A

Today's readings show us two different attitudes on the part of people in need. The Exodus story pictures the Israelites in their journey from Egypt to the Promised Land, already wondering if they made a mistake to leave their slavery behind in Egypt, murmuring because their condition was so needy. In the Gospel, the Canaanite woman's encounter with Jesus shows that she had a very different attitude toward her desperate need for the healing of her daughter. I think that we all show both attitudes at different times in our lives.

The people of Israel were supposed to learn something about God's faithfulness before they reached the land promised to their forefathers. They did not have Abraham's trust in God, who obviously meant that the wilderness experience should teach them that all-important lesson. We can learn from our wilderness experiences, too—from the times when we cannot see how things can possibly work out. God is able!

God does not always answer our prayers immediately nor in the way we expect. We may even begin to think that 1) prayer does not work, 2) God is not interested in our concerns, or 3) that God is angry with us. According to the Bible, the first two can never be true. They are accusing thoughts from our adversary the devil, who wants to persuade us that God does not care. As for the third thought, we might give that a little attention. Jesus said, "Whatever you ask in prayer, believe that you will receive it, and you will. And whenever you stand praying, forgive, if you have anything against anyone" (Mark 11:24, 25a). Jesus puts these two remarkable things together here: forgiveness of others and answers to our prayers. So it doesn't do any harm to ask God, "Am I holding on to something that is displeasing to You and is blocking the answer to my earnest prayer?"

Delays purify our prayers, and help us sort out what it is we truly desire. But delays are not denials. God's Word stands true. The Canaanite woman found it so. And so can we.

In Our Own Language   JULY 14

Isaiah 44:1-8 and Acts 2:1-21

Each one heard them speaking in his own language. ACTS 2:6B

Speech is a very important way of communicating with others. We use it to ask for what we want, or to express thanks, to teach, to scold, to praise. When we are in a place where we cannot understand what is being said, we tend to feel very uncomfortable and strange.

The story of Pentecost in the second chapter of Acts is one of the most thrilling and exciting in the whole Bible. The disciples were waiting, as they had been instructed by Jesus. Then it happened—bringing strange and wonderful signs that God was moving in a new and powerful way. They all began to praise God in languages they did not understand. Others, hearing the commotion, thought they were drunk. But no, this was not intoxication. This was a great new inner joy that came from having the love of God shed abroad in their hearts by the Holy Spirit! We too can have that same inner joy and that same love shed abroad in our hearts. For, as we are told in today's Scripture, "The promise is . . . to all them that are afar off, even as many as the Lord our God shall call." And that includes you and me!

There is another wonderful thing about this story. Each person was able to hear about the love of God in his own language. God speaks to us in terms that we can understand and receive at the very deepest level. We do not have to have great learning. We do not have to understand great myster- ies. For God, by the Holy Spirit, is taking the one story of Jesus, and making it a way of bringing us all back into union with himself and with one another.

I believe he wants to shed his love abroad in our hearts

today in a fuller, deeper way than ever, so that we might have the same inner joy that made those early disciples burst out in praises on that first Pentecost. May it be so for you.

Then You Shall Know   JULY 15

Exodus 16:2-15 and Matthew 15:21-28

At twilight you shall eat flesh, and in the morning you shall be filled with bread; then you shall know that I am the Lord your God.   EXODUS 16:12B

The people of Israel had embarked on a very great adventure. They had been persuaded to leave the safety of their slave-life in Egypt, to venture forth to a land they had heard about but had never seen. Moses assured them that God was leading them forth to undreamed-of freedom. They had been taught about God from their childhood, and they had heard about his promises to their forefathers. So God was not a stranger to them.

The trip turned out to be anything but simple! Their belief in God did not prepare them for all they met, and soon they were discouraged and wanted to go back to their old life.

God was patient with his people, and he is patient with us today. When we long to get back to the "good old days," we are really saying that God is wrong in having life move on. But life is a pilgrimage, and we Christians journey by faith to the Promised Land, very much like the Israelites of old.

God intends that we shall learn to trust him more by learning more perfectly who he is. We come to know him through all our experiences, good and bad, happy and sad.

The Israelites were given quail to eat because they murmured against God. They were given manna, the bread from heaven, because God loved them. The quail made them sick, but the manna gave them strength for their journey. In both cases they were learning to know God.

Think of how God has blessed you and provided for you when you were unable to provide for yourself. He has always been with you and is still with you today, using all the things that come into your life to help you know him more fully. He is revealed in his Son Jesus in all his compassion and mercy. The story of your life and mine is our journey from darkness to light, from slavery to our old selves to our freedom as God's dear children.

Remembering How We Were Led   JULY 16

Deuteronomy 8:1-10 and John 6:37-51

And you shall remember all the way which the Lord your God has led you . . . that he might humble you . . . and let you hunger, and fed you with manna . . . that he might make you know. . . .   DEUTERONOMY 8:2-3

Life is a journey, a pilgrimage. We may not move very far from where we were born, but things change, and we change. Israel had come a long way from where it started. It had left Egypt in a hurry, just ahead of Pharaoh's troops. It had left Egypt as a slave people, with little understanding of what it would mean to live as responsible, free people in the Promised Land. And the journey wound around through many turns, with many stops and delays, as the people were being prepared for their new life. It took forty years!

That's not such a surprising thing if you think of life as

a journey from slavery to freedom, from infancy to maturity. For in our journey we too are learning and being trained to live as God's children. This is not something we were born with, for we are all self-centered by nature, rather than God-centered. And so the Father lovingly trains, leads, chastens, corrects, feeds, nourishes and encourages us as we go along.

In this Deuteronomy passage, the writer says that Israel should remember "all the way which the Lord your God has led you." That's good advice for us, if we look through eyes of faith and thanksgiving. Can you perceive that God's hand was over all your journey? Can you believe that he has always provided for you, and will still provide? That there was always enough strength to get through the hard places, and that there will always be enough strength for whatever lies ahead? That's what remembering should do. Jesus wants us to keep on keeping on, looking up, not losing heart—until we have finished our journey.

Armed for the Fight   JULY 17

Romans 5:12-21 and Matthew 4:1-11

Then Jesus was led up by the Spirit into the wilderness to be tempted by the devil.   MATTHEW 4:1

The first thing that strikes me about this text is this: It tells us that Jesus was led by the Holy Spirit into the desert to be tempted. I don't know how you read that, but it sounds to me like the Gospel is telling us that he was led there in order to be tempted. I believe it means that this was a testing time that the Spirit, obeying the Father's will, was leading Jesus to accept.

Temptation and testing are very closely related. If Jesus is going to be our Sacrifice for sin, the perfect man offering perfect obedience to God as no human being ever had since the Fall in the Garden of Eden, then he would have to undergo the test. That temptation would only be symbolic of the testing of his whole life, for at every turn he chose the Father's will. He met temptation but did not give in to it.

Jesus came "pre-prayed" into this experience, and he was armed for the fight. But he used the same weapons available to us. We, too, can pre-pray, as he teaches us in the Lord's Prayer. We can immerse our minds in the great truths of God's love and mercy and be prepared to fight against those elements in our nature that drag us down.

Jesus faced many tests, and the greatest one was facing the Cross. You and I face many tests and the greatest one is what we do with things we cannot control—our health, our future, our circumstances. These are the testing places, and Jesus shows us how to meet them and not let them destroy us. More than that, he not only shows us how to meet them, but when we are facing them, he is here with us to help us make the right choices. I do so want to make the right choices so that when the test is over, he can say, "Well done, good and faithful servant." Don't you?

The Path of Life   JULY 18

Psalm 16:5-11 and John 20:19-31

*Thou dost show me the path of life; in thy presence there
is fullness of joy; in thy right hand are pleasures for evermore.*
PSALM 16:11

Are there not times in your life and mine when, discouraged with circumstances beyond our control—perhaps
grieving over the loss of someone near and dear to us, facing
sickness or bodily weakness—that we wonder "Is this the
path of life?"

The psalmist who penned the words of the beautiful
16th Psalm knew what it was to be afraid, to feel lonely, to
face the dark times of life. He began by saying, "In thee I
take my refuge. . . . I have no good apart from thee" (Psalm
16:1-2). Yet knowing the dark times, he cries out, "Thou
didst not give me up to Sheol." We can see in those words a
dire prophecy about Jesus, who would go down into the
dark of death and the grave. But it was not possible that the
grave should hold him. He would burst out with the irre-
sistible power of divine life. We can see in those words, too,
a description of what we sometimes experience, when our
souls really are "in Hell," the hell of despair, the hell of fear,
of anxiety, or resentment or pain. In those moments, long or
brief though they be, we feel that God is far away, and we
taste a little of what hell is—the absence of God.

Thanks be to God, he is a caring, patient, steadying God.
We do not have to depend even on our own ability to hold
on to him, or to raise us up out of our gloom by ourselves.
He is the lifter up of the fallen, the helper of the helpless, the
God who raises the dead!

The God who raised Jesus from the dead can come into

the quiet places, the hard places, the seemingly impossible places, and instruct us "in the night." We can choose to bless him, to be glad, to rest in his power, because we are the children of his love. Jesus has won the victory over all these enemies we face in ourselves, and if we will turn to him in our need, pour out our hearts to him, he will come and help us. All his people through the ages have found it so, and we, too, can walk in that path of life, finding that in his presence there is fullness of joy, and pleasures of which the world knows nothing.

Our True Identity   JULY 19

I Thessalonians 5:1-11 and Matthew 25:14-30

For God has not destined us for wrath, but to obtain salvation through our Lord Jesus Christ. I THESS. 5:9

After we have spent the years of our lives earning a living or raising a family, pursuing our ambitions this way and that, it comes down to this: What is my true identity? Who am I, really? I read something like this passage from Paul's letter to the Thessalonians, and my heart "leaps up" (as the poet said) at that good news: "God has not destined us for wrath."

I think many of us spent much of our lives trying to make ourselves "worthy." But then we reach a time when people do not "need" us in quite the way they once did. The children are out on their own, making their own decisions. Companies (or churches) we once were vitally involved in, continue to function without us. And that leaves us free to ask some really basic questions about life and its meaning.

Paul wanted the Christians in Thessalonica to know that

God's will for them was good. They had their difficulties, and they knew what it meant to suffer. But if they could keep in their hearts the sure knowledge that God loved them and had destined them to an eternal life of blessed fulfillment, they would be able to stand in the face of trouble.

And so can we. If we let the knowledge of God's great love for us "get into" our hearts, it can make all the difference in the way we face each day. I know that to be true, and I'm finding it to be true in my own life—more and more. We can find, because of God's love and the presence of the Holy Spirit abiding in our hearts, that every day is meant to be a day of hope, a day when we look for and find the reality of God's love to us. That is what I hope for and pray for each one of you.

Rivers in the Desert   JULY 20

Isaiah 43:16-21 and Philippians 3:8-14

Behold I am doing a new thing; . . . I will make a way in the wilderness and rivers in the desert; . . . for I give water in the wilderness, rivers in the desert, to give drink to my chosen people, the people whom I formed for myself, that they might declare my praise. ISAIAH 43:19-21

All of us have these desert times in our lives. They are times when life seems to lose its zest, when the "kick" has gone out of it. It may be that the desert is so dry, so discouraging, that we begin to wonder if we'll make it through at all.

This verse speaks wonderfully to such times as this. God is quite aware of how things are with us, and he is not indifferent to our need. And so this marvelous promise, right in the midst of his rebuke to his disobedient people, that he will supply what we cannot supply ourselves.

The desert is a quiet place, away from things that crowd out our awareness of God. The desert also stretches in its silence, harsh and unfriendly though it is. It is open to the sky and stars at night, and makes us aware in a new way of the glory and wonder of God. That is something like "water in the desert."

God has what every one of us needs. The river of his grace and love are always flowing. There are no circumstances so dry that we cannot refresh ourselves at the Fountain of Life.

A Message of Comfort   JULY 21

Isaiah 40:1-11 and II Peter 3:8-15A

Comfort, comfort my people, says your God. Speak tenderly to Jerusalem and cry to her that her warfare is ended, that her iniquity is pardoned. . . . The grass withers, the flower fades, but the word of the Lord endures forever. ISAIAH 40:1, 2A AND 8

Christians look at life realistically, not through some "rose colored" glasses. We face the fact that life on this earth is temporary. It has a beginning and an end. It is a precious gift given to us by a loving Father who chose to share life with us, and bestowed it on us. We may have used it well or we may have wasted it in pursuing false goals. Obviously Israel, to whom Isaiah is speaking in the Old Testament Scripture, had made many wrong choices. So have I. So have you. Some of the choices we made we made in ignorance. Others we made willfully, because we wanted this or that out of life. And we may feel, as life draws nearer its end, that

God is angry at us. The prophet says, "Not so!" Forgiveness has been provided by the sacrifice of Jesus Christ on the cross for us. God chooses to forgive us, and his message is "Comfort, comfort my people."

So if you are uneasy about God in your life, I bid you hear this gracious word. It is for those who need comfort. And I think that is all of us.

I am reminded of the way people report going to their 50th high school reunions. They have to carry an old picture of themselves in order to be recognized, and they have the same difficulty recognizing old schoolmates. "Change and decay." The prophet says, "The grass withers, the flower fades." That is a simple fact of life, and there is something very sad when a person will not accept the fact that faces and flowers do fade. But we can say, "So what? We don't look 18 any more, but there is a beauty that comes with living, suffering, and aging that could not be there at 18! The word of the Lord endures forever. In the "golden years" his word is still true. And what is it? "I have loved you with an everlasting love." That love will not, cannot change, because God does not change. He cares for us, and wants us to continue to find rest in that changeless love.

Living Our Identity   JULY 22

I John 3:1-3 and John 10:11-18

Beloved, we are God's children NOW.   I JOHN 3:2A

When I was young, my mother used to say, "Now, son, remember who you are." What can this mean to us in the light of today's text? Three things come to mind. First, we are beloved. We are not orphans, discards on the ash-heap of life. God loves us, and his love is the very foundation of our existence. Because he set his love upon us, we have been given life. Beyond mere physical life, he has revealed his Son Jesus to us. We are a chosen nation, a holy people, God's own people (I Peter 2:9). This is our heritage. We did not earn it, we do not deserve it—but it is ours anyway, to receive.

Second, God calls us his children, part of his family. Look at some of the Scriptures which invite us to think of God this way: "You have one Father in heaven" (Matthew 23:9b). "You must be perfect as your Father in heaven is perfect" (Matthew 5:48). "Can a woman forget her sucking child, that she should have no compassion on the son of her womb? Even these may forget, yet I will not forget you" (Isaiah 49:15).

Third, we are not only beloved, not only does God call us his children, we are called to live out who we are, to remember who we are. Others may despair. We cannot. Others may indulge in self-centeredness, thinking only of their own welfare, their own petty needs and comfort, their likes and dislikes. We cannot. We are called to live like God's family members, to behave as those who share his likeness. Our pattern is Jesus Christ. Other examples are the blessed souls living and dead who try to live like him by his grace, and inspire us to imitate them. It does not matter what circumstance surrounds us, we can live as those who know who we are. We are God's children now. Let that thought encourage you, strengthen you, and fill you with joy.

Faith and Hope   JULY 23

Psalm 23 and Hebrews 11:1-12

*And what is faith? Faith gives assurance to our hopes, and makes
us certain of realities we do not see.*   HEBREWS 11:1 (NEB)

Faith is a gift. I cannot make myself believe something I do
not believe. Yet I can put myself into "the way of faith,"
and pray for faith when I do not have it. Like the man who
came to Jesus with his son for healing, we can pray, "Lord,
I believe. Help my unbelief!"

Putting ourselves into "the way of faith" may involve
looking hard at the things that block us from believing.
When we make bad choices against the light we have, we
violate our consciences, and we harden our hearts against
faith. Doubts come easily. Faith built on experience helps us
to look at the world with "faith-eyes." We know that the visible and the immediate are not the whole story. We know
that some things are worth fighting for, some things worth
dying for, things we cannot see.

I stood in the American Cemetery in Cambridge,
England, where 30 acres have been deeded to the United
States as a place of commemoration for those who died at
sea, in the air and in England during World War II. I looked
at the 3,000 grave sites and saw the names of other thousands of young men and women who died far from home
and family. For what? For something that could not be
"seen," but was worthy of sacrifice. One cannot walk along
the beautiful "Wall of Memory" and be unmoved.

Faith "gives assurance to our hopes." What would life be
without hope? And yet for all of us, it will come to an end.
Sometimes the end is accompanied with suffering, always
with the pain of parting. Is there hope beyond that sadness?
Faith gives assurance that there is. The 11th chapter of

Hebrews tells us of the heroes who have gone on before us, "seeing the invisible." We could add many more names to the list. Will ours be added to it one day?

God's Faithfulness JULY 24

II Timothy 2:8-15 and Luke 17:11-19

*If we are faithless, he remains faithful—for he
cannot deny himself.* II TIMOTHY 2:13

The older I get, the more wonderful the privilege seems to be able to write or speak about the faithfulness of God. For every day, every week, there are new evidences of that unchanging faithfulness of your heavenly Father and mine.

It is good, as the Bible reminds us, to rehearse the blessings God has bestowed on us. You remember how the people of Israel, after witnessing that most amazing miracle of crossing the Red Sea on dry ground, went three days journey into the wilderness. When difficulty arose, they began to accuse Moses of leading them out there to destroy them. How quickly they had forgotten the faithfulness of God!

Jesus healed ten lepers in today's Gospel reading. Nine of them were so excited about the change in their condition that they forgot to turn back to say "Thank you" to the one who had made it all possible. Gratitude and remembering go hand in hand.

Friends who are going through a hard time sometimes come to talk about their feelings. Something I do is recommend that they spend time thanking God for what they know he has done for them, to be specific in naming the blessings he has bestowed. When all is said and done, he remains faithful, for he cannot deny himself. And on that truth we can rely.

Waiting for God   JULY 25

Isaiah 64:1-9 and I Corinthians 1:3-9

From of old no one has heard or perceived by the ear,
no eye has seen a God besides thee, who works
for those who wait for him.   ISAIAH 64:4

Waiting is hard. It is hard work. Isaiah knew this when he wrote today's text. He was in a waiting time.

Paul too knew a lot about waiting, and the Christians at Corinth had their times of waiting too. They needed comfort. That means they were *uncomfortable*. We know that those first generations of Christians had many reasons to need comfort. They had put their trust in Jesus Christ, and many people felt that they were foolish indeed to place their hope of heaven in him. But Paul was given the grace to reassure them that indeed this Jesus was the Christ whom God had promised for many ages. Moreover, the Holy Spirit was active in their midst, and there were many evidences that God helps those who wait for him.

All of us experience waiting times. Things are not the way we had hoped they would be. It may be difficult in many ways to see God's hand in our present circumstance. But our Scriptures today are speaking to you and me in our waiting. What are you waiting for? Are you really waiting for God? If so, I believe with all my heart that you will not be disappointed. He is faithful and mindful of those who rely on him. He may not come when we would like him to appear. He may not perform the miracle we think would be so important and such a blessing. But he *will* come in answer to prayer and faith. That has been my own experience in some very hard, dark times. When the darkness passes and the light shines again, how much more heartily do we say,

"The Lord is faithful! His mercy endures forever."

Waiting time is a time for battle, a time to affirm what we know from experience, and what we have learned from the lives of others. Let us not waste these waiting times, but let them become occasions of sending our roots deeper into the goodness and faithfulness of God.

To the Close of the Age   JULY 26

Psalm 8 and Matthew 28:16-20

And lo, I am with you always, to the close of the age.
MATTHEW 28:20B

The last word that Matthew records from the Risen Christ is this Great Commission ("Go") and this solemn promise: "I am with you always."

Most of us are not at the age when we can volunteer to become missionaries to some exotic place (this writer used to think he wanted to be a missionary in South America). Most of us are too timid about sharing our faith that we wouldn't think of going out on the street corner and preaching to passing crowds, or even handing out religious tracts to unwary passersby.

We can, however, give thanks for those who heard and heeded the Great Commission to go and preach the gospel, for in so doing, our own ancestors were reached with the good news of Jesus. And we can continue where we are to witness to his love and pray for those who are "on the firing line," carrying the good news to the hard places at home and abroad.

But what about the latter part of the verse—our text for today? I think we need that word every day. At least I do.

How easy it is to forget that he is faithful and that he is still keeping that promise. No matter where we are, how long our journey has been, what the stumblings and mistakes we have made, he just keeps on keeping his word, "I am with you always."

We get frightened at what we imagine might lie ahead of us on the journey. It is easy to become anxious, and the Lord knows how frail and weak our faith is. So he keeps assuring and reassuring us that he is with us. Is the day a sunny, happy one? He is there with us, rejoicing in our joy. Is the day a dark and difficult one? He is there, giving us the strength we need to get through it.

Yes, he is with us, the same yesterday, today and forever. He always keeps his word.

Our Needless Fears   JULY 27

II Timothy 1:1-14 and Luke 7:5-10

For God did not give us a spirit of timidity but a spirit of power and love and self control.   II TIMOTHY 1:7

As we go through life, we are learning about the relationship between faith and fear. The disciples asked Jesus to increase their faith, and he reminded them that if they had even as much "as a grain of mustard seed," they could remove mountains.

I think for many of us those mountains are mountains of fear. Many of us try to hide our fear by not talking about it, hoping it will go away. But fear can make us very defensive and self-enclosed. Jesus offers you and me a better way of handling our life. He offers us his own presence and understanding, and wants to communicate his love and concern to us. He can hear our faintest cry, our call for help, our confession that we are afraid.

Paul says that we have been given a spirit of power, love and self-control. That means that in the face of every danger, every threat to our health and well-being, even in the face of the fact that our earthly life will end one day, we can cast away needless fear. By exercising our faith, we can deal with our fears. They do not have to have control over us. They will rise up, for we are human. But with the grace and help of the Lord we can deal with them and not be defeated by them.

And They Believed   JULY 28

I Corinthians 1:18-25 and John 2:13-22

When therefore he was raised from the dead, his disciples remembered that he had said this; and they believed the scripture and the word which Jesus had spoken. JOHN 2:22

The disciples were with Jesus day and night for about three years. They listened to his words, they saw the miracles he performed. The lame walked, the blind had their sight restored, the deaf heard, and even the dead were raised. Yet we know that when his great hour of trial came, "they all forsook him and fled." They were made of the same clay that we are, and that is why their experiences are so helpful to us.

Here in today's Gospel, Jesus has an encounter with the vested interests who were turning the Temple into a house of merchandise. Jesus, manifesting the heart and care of God, showed the only act of "physical violence" we have recorded in the Gospel. He took a cord and made a whip of it, and drove out the moneychangers, overturning their tables and dispersing the doves and animals waiting to be sold. Naturally, they were not pleased! In the discussion that followed, he made a kind of word play on the term "temple," and predicted his own resurrection. The whole incident came back to the disciples' minds after he had been crucified and had risen again.

The point made here was that the resurrection confirmed his word and the promise of Scripture. So they were able then to place their faith on solid ground: the fact of the resurrection. We have that same ground of faith. God is not limited by our horizons. He not only created this world and gave it existence. He raises the dead. If we could really and truly believe that, we could do what the martyrs and saints have done in all ages: face any foe and come away victorious. "O for a faith that will not shrink, though pressed by every foe!"

Three Encouraging Words   July 29

II Corinthians 5:6-10 and Mark 4:26-34

We are always of good courage . . . for we walk by faith. . . . We make it our aim to please him. II Corinthians 5:6A, 7A AND 9B

Paul gives these three great words of encouragement to the Corinthians. Their faith may have been as small as that tiny, pepper-like speck which Jesus was talking about in his parable. The first word is this: we are always of good courage. To be of good courage is to have firmness of mind and purpose, throwing aside the fear that everyone has. Courage is the quality which keeps us going on in spite of everything. We all need courage to see us through the hard places. Christ within the heart is the supplier of that firmness we need. If we keep close to him, danger cannot overturn us. "We are always of good courage."

The second word is this: We walk by faith, not by sight. God is very wise and merciful in allowing us to remember the past and have faith for the future. He is teaching us to trust him rather than our own eyesight. There is always enough inner light to choose the next step he asks us to take, and grace enough to meet present need. We do not need to see the future, and would not know what to do with it if we could. So in his mercy, he calls us to walk by faith, not by sight.

The third encouraging word is this: We make it our aim to please him. That is Paul's secret of peace. Since he had to face difficult circumstances every day (circumstances he could not change), he kept his heart at peace by making it his aim to keep Christ very near. When he is present, there is peace within. Under the stormy surface of life, he brings an inner calm which we all need and deeply desire. These encouraging words are meant to lift us out of ourselves and into his serenity and peace.

Eyes to See Him   JULY 30

Exodus 34:29-35 and Luke 9:28-36

Now Peter and those who were with him were heavy with sleep, and when they wakened, they saw his glory. . . .   LUKE 9:32

The disciples had been following Jesus for many months, and perhaps they were tempted to think that they had seen it all. Lepers were healed, paralytics leapt for joy, water changed to wine, one lunch served more than 5,000 people, and the dead were raised. Now he was taking Peter, James and John to a nearby hilltop, to pray. This would not have been unusual for them. But life is never "normal" to a follower of Jesus Christ. Just when we think we've seen it all, he has something more to show us.

With no announcement or fanfare, Jesus was suddenly transfigured before the very eyes of his disciples. He shone like the sun, and, as Luke tells us, Peter, James and John "saw his glory." With no introduction, Moses and Elijah, those giants of the Old Testament, "appeared in glory" and talked with Jesus. And the voice of God declared from the cloud: "This is my Son, my Chosen; listen to him!" What only a few moments before had seemed ordinary, became a supernatural experience with the living God! Those disciples would never be the same after that encounter. They would think of it for many years to come, and Peter would write of it to his readers (II Peter 1:16-18).

There are many lessons we might gather from this event. First, as human beings we very easily become creatures of routine. In such a context we are tempted to think that that is all there is to living. Jesus would have us to know otherwise. No matter how long we have been living, or for how many years we have been disciples of Jesus Christ, there is still more for us to see and learn about him. Every day can bring a fresh encounter with Jesus—through prayer, through the Scriptures, through what a friend or even a stranger may say to us, through the sight of a bird, or a child, or a picture hanging on the wall.

If we are open to such encounters, we become instruments by which God reveals himself to others. Peter told others of his experience, and Moses' face shone with brightness after he met God. The more our eyes are opened to see Jesus, the more others will see him reflected in our countenance. When we see his glory, it is we who are transfigured! Let us pray today for eyes to see him.

What Shall We Say to These Things? July 31

Romans 8:31-39 and Matthew 14:13-21

What then shall we say to this? If God is for us, who can be against us? Romans 8:31

Paul is talking about the sufferings we are all called to undergo in this earthly pilgrimage. This whole chapter (Romans 8) centers on this concern, because even then there were some who felt that if they loved God, they should be delivered from all suffering.

Now we know that this is not true. All of us, believers and non-believers, have suffering of various kinds in our lives. The difference, it seems to me, is that "All things work together for good to those who love him. . . ." And just a few lines further on Paul names some of these things that work together for good to those who love God: tribulation, distress, persecution, famine, nakedness, peril and sword. That doesn't exactly sound like a great group of blessings, does it?

What "things" are in your life and mine that we have to struggle with? Not all suffering is physical pain, though that is the lot of some. I think one of the greatest hindrances to our realization of the truth of this passage is our easy descent into self-pity. It is always there, waiting to be chosen at a moment's notice. "Why me? Why has this come to me?" And away we go down that slippery slide into the "slough of despond" (as Bunyan called it). Once there, it takes some effort to get out. We may even need someone to speak sharply to us and remind us that such a place is no fit place for a child of God!

The Giving Father

For God so loved the world that he gave his one and only son, that whoever believes in him shall not perish but have eternal life.

JOHN 3:16 (NIV)

Onward Christian Soldiers

My minister friend of twenty years was an active, vibrant individual who loved the Lord, people and sports, and served as Chaplain of the Fire Department. His life took a shocking turn when, after noticing some numbness in his hands and change in his speech, he went to the Lahey Clinic near Boston. There he was diagnosed as having ALS, better known as Lou Gehrig's disease, with an average life expectancy of two years.

Over the next nineteen months, his condition deteriorated, first slowly, then more rapidly, with his speech becoming more and more slurred until he was no longer able to speak and was confined to a wheelchair, dependent on others to take him where he needed to go. One of the most difficult times for him came when he was no longer able to serve Holy Communion, because his hand muscles had atrophied so much he couldn't handle the elements. He had his down times, yet through it all he had a ready smile and a quick thumbs-up. Frequently, he would scribble on his pad, "God is good."

Personally, it was very difficult to see my friend's condition deteriorate, forcing me to deal with my own mortality, to see how frail life is. But living through his suffering brought a change in me, for I began to have a more grateful heart, and others commented that I was more patient and less self-centered.

When he became confined to a wheelchair, I took him to church and wheeled him around to other places on his daily "walk." What began as a duty for me soon became a privilege, as I saw him wrestle with the reality of being completely dependent on others. It reminded me of Jesus' words to Peter, "When you were younger you dressed yourself and went where you wanted; but when you are old you will stretch out your hands and someone else will dress you and lead you where you do not want to go."

Over time I saw my friend transformed and softened as he became a person with a sweet, gentle spirit. He always wanted more of this life but more than that, he wanted God's will. Shortly before his death, he asked to have *Pilgrim's Progress* read to him. He especially liked the chapter in which Christian is approaching the heavenly city.

On the night before he died, several of us were with him in his room. He kept reaching out and pointing, as if he wanted us to see what he was seeing—beyond this life. Was it angels beckoning, or Jesus reaching out his hand to lead him on?

There was no question that he knew where he was going and he was ready. His funeral was a time of rejoicing for a life fully lived, and for the certain knowledge that he is in the Father's house of many rooms.

Paul Varga

Courtesy of Dan Bosler/Tony Stone Images

Abounding in Hope　　　　　　　　AUGUST 1

Isaiah 11:1-10 and Romans 15:4-13

May the God of hope fill you with all joy and peace in believing,
so that by the power of the Holy Spirit you may abound in hope.
ROMANS 15:13

When I read words like this, I am ashamed of how weak and limited my own hope seems to be. Think back to those days when Paul was carrying the gospel of Jesus Christ to the "corners" of the Roman Empire. There was no "worldwide" church to support his preaching. There were no 2,000 years of Christian testimony to back up his preaching. There was just the unquenchable faith that he had found the "words of eternal life," and that Jesus had changed everything—present and future. Knowing that Jesus had died and risen again made all the difference for Paul, and for the thousands of people who became Christians under his ministry.

Paul's hope was not a secular, materialistic hope. Today we are so geared to think of instant solutions, and wonder why we can't solve the problems that continue to wrack the world. All those things existed in Paul's day as well. So whatever hope they had was something greater than just correcting world or social conditions.

What was this hope for which Paul prays? Part of it, at least, is stated in our text: "joy and peace in believing." It is the return we get from having that living hope in our hearts. The hope is grounded in "the God of hope." He and he alone is able to carry us through all the dangers and difficulties of this mortal life—no matter who we are! He it is who has come to our rescue, entered our broken, bleeding, sinful world with a message of love and life. He does not turn away from the ugliness he sees in the world—or in us. Rather, he invites us to believe that by his grace and with the power of the Holy Spirit we can begin to live more faithfully and more completely as children of God.

One day the world will know who God is. One day every knee will bow before him who created all things. One day Jesus Christ will be acknowledged as the Lord of lords and King of kings. That is part of our Christian hope. I believe it shall be even as it has been told. I believe that it will come to pass as God has promised. And, in the meantime, the God of hope offers to fill my heart—and yours—"with all joy and peace in believing."

Rejoice, Be Patient, Be Constant   AUGUST 2

Matthew 16:21-28 and Romans 12:9-12

*Rejoice in your hope, be patient in tribulation,
be constant in prayer.* ROMANS 12:12

The Apostle Paul says in his letter to the Romans, "I thank my God through Jesus Christ for all of you, because your faith is proclaimed in all the world" (Romans 1:8). Christians everywhere were impressed that these people were standing firm for their faith, even in the heart of the empire, Rome itself. We know that Christians were frequently persecuted just because they were Christians. There are many places in the world where that is still true, and we would do well to remember our brothers and sisters in our prayers.

Paul's advice in our text is good for us, no matter what circumstances we may be facing.

First, *rejoice in your hope*. Don't complain. The believing heart knows that there is always room for rejoicing. Someone has said, "We have read the last chapter of the story, and we know how it comes out." That is our hope. Our hope is in what God has promised to bring to completion. Life is not finished, and neither are we. We have a hope because of Jesus Christ. We can nourish our hope and rejoice in it, or we can neglect it and forget that it is ours.

Second, *be patient in tribulation*. The dictionary defines tribulation as "distress or suffering resulting from oppression or persecution"; also, "a trying experience." In my experience, our "oppression" often comes from thoughts and feelings within, not just from what others are doing to us. So when "tribulation" comes, we are told to "be patient." St. Teresa is quoted as having often said, "This, too, will pass." Remember that when you are feeling down. It *will* pass. Be patient.

Third, *be constant in prayer*. That, I think, is the key. Prayer is like water to a plant. If a plant isn't watered, it will die. It must have water to live. And so with our souls. If we neglect this awesome privilege and responsibility, our soul shrinks and shrivels to a shadow of what it should be. Don't let any day go by without having a heart-to-heart talk with your heavenly Father. Remember that he loves you and waits for you to come to him.

Temptations   AUGUST 3

Genesis 9:8-17 and Mark 1:9-15

And he was in the wilderness forty days,
tempted by Satan.   MARK 1:13

We learn some important things about Jesus and about ourselves as we look at these accounts of his temptations in the wilderness. First of all, they came when he was making important decisions about what he was going to do in carrying out his mission. He knew who he was, and he already knew that the way led to the Cross. But there were decisions to be made, and his fasting and prayer time in the wilderness was a decision time. The temptations came in the form of allurements or suggestions that 1) he turn stones into bread, 2) win the kingdoms of the world by the wrong means, and 3) show who he was by throwing himself down from the pinnacle of the temple in faith that God would protect him.

The first temptation was to be self-sufficient, to provide for himself. And that has always seemed like a good thing to most of us—we have prized our independence and lack of reliance on others! But when the devil suggested this in Jesus' ear, he replied, "Get behind me, Satan! Man shall not live by bread alone [by what we can provide for ourselves], but by every word that proceeds from God." God is the provider and we need to recognize that. We live by God's power, by God's sustenance, by God's provision.

The second temptation was to power and possessions. Most of us like both! But Jesus said no to this one, and chose to serve only God. In another place he said, "You cannot serve God and mammon." We must keep our priorities straight, or we will end up serving a dead, lifeless god.

The third temptation was to presume upon God's mercy and care. Some of us do that by eating or drinking too much (or too little!), eating the wrong things, not taking proper exercise, or by harboring bad attitudes and thoughts that eat away at the body's strength like acid. We wouldn't get up on a tall building and jump off, but we presume to take poor care of our bodies and expect God to take care of us.

Jesus recognized temptation for what it was—an attempt of the enemy to throw him off course and destroy his work.

We would be better off if we could recognize when we are being tempted to go against what God would have us do, so that we could resist such thoughts.

Out of his temptations, Jesus grew in obedience and matured in his relationship with the Father. If we meet our temptations in the right spirit, learn to recognize them for what they are, and fight against them, calling on the help and energy of God to aid us, we, too, can grow and mature as children of God.

Called to Stand AUGUST 4

Ephesians 6:10-20 and Mark 7:1-8, 14-15, 21-23

And having done all, to stand. EPHESIANS 6:13B

The word "stand" appears three times in this short passage from Ephesians, and the word "withstand" makes it four. So the apostle is really concerned that we sense the importance of "standing." It's an interesting word, quite different from another image we run into in the Bible: the words "run," or "race," or "walk."

Our standing must be, says the apostle, "against the wiles of the devil." The word "wiles" is not one we commonly use, so I looked it up for my own edification. The thesaurus gives "artifice, cunning, contrivance, scheme, and trick" as some of the synonyms. Think about that in terms of your own life, and the way things sometimes appear to you. The devil, our adversary, is very clever, and never comes to us with his real image showing. Instead, he insinuates into our minds little thoughts—jealousies, resentments, vain wishes, discouragements—all intended to get us to give up in our struggle to stand for what God is and what God has done in our lives. If he can just get us to feel that faith is a mistake, that there is no use really trying to love God, to believe in him, to trust him for today and tomorrow, he has accomplished his goal.

But our passage gives us the solution to these deceptive, tricky thoughts and feelings. "Put on the whole armor of God," we are told. Then the passage tells us what that means: the breastplate of righteousness, our feet shod with the equipment of the gospel of peace, the shield of faith, the helmet of salvation and the sword of the Spirit, "which is the word of God."

A breastplate was an important protection for the soldier in Paul's day. It protected the heart. When he says we should put on "the breastplate of righteousness," he certainly does not mean our own "self" righteousness, but the righteousness that we have by faith in Jesus Christ.

All the other images here suggest a state of alertness, of the knowledge that we are in a spiritual battle with the powers of darkness. Knowing that these feelings and temptations are "the wiles of the devil" will help us to make better choices, to "fight the good fight with all our might," and to see that we have the necessary equipment to win the battle. May it be so for you.

A Tested Foundation

Isaiah 28:14-22 and Luke 13:22-30

Behold, I am laying in Zion for a foundation, a stone,
a tested stone, a precious cornerstone, a sure foundation.
He who believes will not waiver. ISAIAH 28:16
(MIXED TRANSLATION)

In our personal lives, this question needs to be raised: On what foundation are we building, on what basis do we pin our faith and our hope? As we face some of the harder times of life, these experiences tend to unveil or uncover what inner foundations we are building on. For example, a former parishioner of mine faced serious heart surgery. Before the operation, however, she "went to pieces," because she had no inner trust in God. In that same parish, a bitter old lady was afraid her money would run out before she died. In her beautiful, comfortable, well above-average home, she lived in misery and fear.

As Christians, our faith rests on a sure foundation, which God himself has laid for us. We learn of it through the entire Old Testament as God progressively reveals himself to his people. And we find it perfectly in Jesus Christ. Paul said, "There is no other foundation than that which is laid in Jesus Christ our Lord." We know for sure who it is when we remember that God raised him from death and opened the gates of eternal life to all who believe in him. This is the eternal, ever-new Good News to us all. We do not have to live on the shaky foundation of our own home-made religions or philosophies. God has provided something better.

This foundation will stand every test. The saints, apostles, prophets and martyrs of every age have testified that God has not failed them. Life cannot throw anything at us that can shake us from this faith, if we choose Jesus Christ. It is

a heart matter, a matter hidden from the storms and difficulties of the world, where we can hold communion with
him, find strength for each hour, find healing for our hurts,
forgiveness for our sins, and hope for the future. What a
foundation indeed!

Speak Lord: We Hear   AUGUST 6

I Samuel 3:1-10 and John 1:35-51

And the Lord came and stood forth, calling as at other times,
"Samuel! Samuel!" And Samuel said, "Speak, for thy
servant hears."   I SAMUEL 3:10

The story of the child Samuel has always fascinated readers
of the Bible. It reveals very clearly that "in many and
various ways God spoke of old to our fathers," in the same
way that he speaks to us today: by an inner Voice that may
at times be very strong indeed. The story also reminds us of
how a mother gave back to God the very blessing he had
given her—taking the child for whom she had prayed back
to the tabernacle to be dedicated to a lifetime of service to
the Lord. That is a lesson for all of us—not only to give our
children back to God, but to give back to God every gift he
has given us, to be used for his purposes, not according to
our own ambitions or wishes.

When Samuel first heard the voice of the Lord, he
assumed it was the voice of Eli. When he went to the old
priest, Eli did not understand what was happening, so he
sent the child back to bed. But Eli had had enough dealing
with God to recognize finally that this was not just a dream
young Samuel was having. God was speaking. And so he
instructed Samuel how to respond if the voice came again.

As I read that story, I wondered how many times I have missed hearing what God was saying to me because I assumed it was someone else. In Hebrews it says, "In many and various ways God spoke of old to our fathers by the prophets." The message came to people through someone else. And you and I may miss what God is saying to us through another person, because God does use different people to speak to us. But if we believe that God is in charge of our lives, that he is concerned for where we are and what is going on in us, we will do well to listen for his voice coming through others. After all, Balaam the prophet was spoken to by his donkey in the Bible—and the donkey said just what Balaam needed to hear at that moment!

The important thing is a willingness to hear "the still small voice" or the word being given through someone else. How many lives have been turned in a good direction by a faithful teacher who said the right word at the right time! When we go to a religious service with the attitude of listening—not to hear how good the sermon is, but what the Lord is saying to us, it is amazing how much good we can take away from such a service.

It is exciting when we begin really to listen to what God will say to us, and to know that he is not silent, passive or indifferent. He really cares about you. He has something to say to you because he loves you. There is no need to be afraid that you are going to be strange if you begin to listen to what God may be saying. It simply means turning your inner ear, the ear of your heart and soul, to the sounds of eternity.

God had an important message for Samuel. Alas! Eli still did not hear it, but kept going in the same direction, until he and his disobedient sons came to a tragic end. But the experience was important for Samuel. And for us. Let our attitude be throughout the day, and throughout the waking hours of the night: "Speak, Lord, for I am listening."

The Best News   AUGUST 7

II Chronicles 36:14-23 and John 3:14-21

For God sent the son into the world, not to condemn the world, but that the world might be saved through him.   JOHN 3:17

I write these lines two days after the death of my brother at the age of 57. His was a troubled life in many ways—his marriage failed, he often changed jobs, and for a long period his drinking was out of control. But something happened a few years ago, and his life began to take on a new direction. Then, just a short time ago, he found that he was terminally ill. It was a difficult illness, and when I saw him last, he could communicate only by writing notes.

In the midst of this, instead of being bitter and afraid, he began to express his love to his family and to those to whom he was close. The first words he wrote on a clipboard in the Intensive Care Unit when I visited him were, "I love you." I don't think either of us had used those words to each other before. Another thing he did was to write to those he felt he had wronged, and ask for their forgiveness. Somehow, in the knowledge that he had but a few days or weeks to live, he was able to reach out to be reconciled and had no difficulty in seeing and admitting where he had been wrong.

All of this is by way of saying that the great good news of the gospel, the best news in the world, is that God is in the business of saving, not of condemning. So often I have felt judgmental towards those whose lives seemed to be disor-dered and destructive, and in my self-righteousness have wanted to straighten them out and get them on the right path! But God does not always do things that way. He waits until we are ready to hear that great, good news that we may not have been able to hear before: that he loves us and cares for us, and that Jesus has come to forgive us and save us. What a comfort it is if we simply, like little children, accept that good news in our hearts.

God's love is so deep and broad that we cannot comprehend it. It is so great that he did not hold back the dearest treasure he had—his only begotten Son. If we avoid him, it is to our own hurt. If we accept him and turn to him, we find that his grace is greater than we could ever have imagined—it reaches even us!

Fear, anxiety, guilt, resentment, bitterness—these have no place in the heart of a child of God who knows the best news in the world. His love is greater, his power is greater and he can replace all these things with a peace that passes knowledge. I saw that miracle in my brother, and I rejoice that he found the Best News and believed it. Let's be open to all God has for us.

Praying with Wisdom   AUGUST 8

I Kings 3:5-12 and Romans 8:26-34

*It pleased the Lord that Solomon had asked this. And God
said to him, "Because you have asked this . . . behold,
I now do according to your word."* I KINGS 3:10-12A

Most of us are afraid to pray bold prayers. We are afraid
they won't go anywhere or achieve anything. So we
protect ourselves from disappointment by not asking. Yet
Jesus bids us boldly to come to the Father with our requests
and make our needs known to him.

Is it not the same with our prayers? On the one hand, we
should have more faith to believe in the goodness of God
and his willingness to hear us when we pray. We do not need
to limit our prayers to the general conditions of the world,
national crises, and such earth-shaking needs. We can ask for
little things, too. Our Heavenly Father hears and has invited
us to make our needs known.

But on the other hand, there is a kind of foolish and
reckless—even selfish—praying that thinks only of what I
want, what I need, what would satisfy my desire. That is not
the kind of praying Jesus taught us to pray. His model prayer
starts with God's agenda—his Name, his will, his kingdom.
So we need to start where he starts.

Solomon prayed the right kind of prayer when he asked
for understanding and wisdom to be a good king. God was
pleased with his request and gave him much wisdom—some
of which is written in the book of Proverbs. God even went
beyond his request and gave him more than he asked. That
is the way God is. He is always more generous than we can
imagine.

But we need wisdom in making our prayers, so that we
fit our requests into his will, his purpose, his rule. We will

not be cheated out of any good things by asking for wisdom to know what to ask for, and to know how to pray. Such wisdom will ennoble our prayers and bring us unexpected pluses which he will add out of his great generosity and love for us.

So let us seek to pray bold and wise prayers, knowing that he knows best!

Not Losing Heart   AUGUST 9

II Timothy 3:14-4:5 and Luke 18:1-8

And [Jesus] told them a parable to the effect that they ought always to pray and not to lose heart.   LUKE 18:1

One of the problems people bring up when they speak of prayer is this: "Why do we not receive an answer to our prayer? Does prayer really work?" And I suppose that no one who has ever taken prayer seriously has escaped such questions. Obviously Jesus was aware of the problem, and even though he challenges us to pray with the most breathtaking promises, he knows full well that the answers will not always come easily or immediately. There will be delays. There will be questions. There will be doubts. Some will even lose heart and stop praying.

And so he tells this little story about the unjust judge and the widow who wouldn't give up. The judge is painted about as bad as you could imagine. He says, "I neither fear God nor regard man." And Jesus makes him as unlike God as possible, in order to make his point. If a judge like that would give in and answer the widow's prayer—*how much more*, he is saying, will God be moved by the persistent prayers of those who come to him!

Yet the delays are there. And we begin to wonder if God is hearing, or just why the answer is so long delayed. It may be that our prayer needs re-examining. Since we are asking God to do something, it is important that our desire and our will be in line with his. Since he loves us with an unqualified love, and since he knows what is best in every circumstance, we would be foolish indeed to insist on something that was contrary to his will. And so it is wise to ask him: Show me your will, Father, in this matter. But having said that, we may also remember that some things will only happen if we pray for them. He waits for his children to ask before he grants them some blessings. So the Lord says we should always pray and not lose heart.

But the Greatest of These　　　AUGUST 10

I Corinthians 13:1-13 and Luke 4:21-30

So faith, hope and love abide, these three; but the
greatest of these is love.　I COR. 13:13

Paul not only encourages us to seek the higher gifts, he gives a beautiful description of the greatest gift of all—one that has been showered on us all: the gift of love.

We all admire people whose faith is so strong that they tackle the impossible and achieve it. We see this faith demonstrated in the efforts of young people to "go for the gold" in the Olympics. Behind the performances we are allowed to watch on our screen are years of effort, painful effort, spurred on by the faith that such efforts will be rewarded.

We also see this gift in those who have the vision and courage to start new things—whether spiritual accomplishments or successful businesses.

But great as faith is, Paul says, love is greater. When faith's object has been achieved, faith is no longer needed. When hope has been realized, hope, in a sense, becomes obsolete. But we never, never outlive the need for love.

Love is not something we achieve, for the truth is, we cannot make ourselves love. And more truth: most of us have a very narrow range of love. But, thanks be to God, we do not have to create love or conjure it up on our own. Love is given to us by the One whose name is Love. "God is love," says John. And by the inner Spirit, God's love has been "shed abroad in our hearts." So what we have to do is to accept God's love, open ourselves to it, and daily seek to have it increase in us. Yes, the greatest of these is love. And that's what life is meant to teach us. May that love fill your heart anew today.

Let Hope Keep You Joyful   AUGUST 11

Romans 12:9-21 and Matthew 18:15-20

Let hope keep you joyful; in trouble stand firm; persist in prayer.
ROMANS 12:12 (NEB)

I cannot imagine a better formula for facing difficult days! And they come from the pen and from the life of one who knew. Paul had certainly seen and experienced more than his share of hardship, pain and rejection. So when he speaks, we know that they are not idle words. I was struck by the three-fold nature of his counsel to us as we face gray days, good days, hard days—and impossible days!

Let hope keep you joyful. It sounds as though we have some choice about it, doesn't it? Hope is not some ethereal thing that comes floating down to us like bubbles. It is a vigorous, strong reality which we are given by God to nurture and nourish in our hearts.

But how can we rejoice in our hope? How can we let it keep us joyful? It will mean that we must rehearse (to ourselves, and possibly to others) the great things that give us reason for hope: that God is with us, that he is for us, and that he will not bring us thus far in order to disappoint or confound us! We can let hope keep us joyful by driving away thoughts of fear and self-pity which we all have from time to time. They do not have to stay with us if we make the choice to rejoice. This may take a little effort—but it's well worth it!

In trouble stand firm. That's the second thing Paul tells us. Sometimes that's all we can do at the moment. We do not have strength to soar with wings of faith. We do not have strength to launch a charge like a battering ram or an army tank. But we can stand firm. That means that even when we seem overwhelmed, we can say to God, "Father, I don't understand, but I trust you." Do not let trouble throw you out of balance. Grasp more firmly the Rock! You know where your help has come from in the past, and he will never, never desert you. That is the truth and you can stand on it. In trouble stand firm.

Persist in prayer. The older versions said, "Be constant in prayer." There is something beautiful about that word "constant." The dictionary defines it as being firm, resolute, faithful, regular, continual, positive. So our text is saying more than just persisting in prayer in a whining, begging way. It is bidding us to continue in prayer in our unshakable expectation that God will give us strength, in perfect confidence and positive assurance that it will be ours.

We are a people of hope. God has planted his hope in our hearts. Do let this cheer you and build you up in your faith. Let hope keep you joyful!

A Stronghold, a Shelter, a Shade   AUGUST 12

Isaiah 25:1-9 and Luke 14:15-24

Thou hast been a stronghold to the poor, a stronghold to the needy in his distress, a shelter from the storm and a shade from the heat. ISAIAH 25:4

Have you ever noticed how many times the Bible speaks of God's concern for the needy, the poor, those who are in trouble? It is as though he is telling us over and over again, that we are the people of his care, the objects of his love.

Isaiah remembers that the good things which God was doing were "plans formed of old, faithful and sure." It is comforting and strengthening to remember that the Lord was planning good for you before you knew you were in need.

I think that the reason for these assurances is that God knows who we are and what we are. He knows that believing is not always easy, that we can easily be cast down by even a small ailment or uncertainty. After a major surgery, I found myself apprehensive over even small developments. I had to confess my fear over and over again to the Lord, because he had brought me through the valley, and his faithfulness never failed. Even knowing that, I still had the humiliation of being afraid instead of being faith-full. So I am praying for more faith and more faith-full-ness.

Today's Gospel tells again of the great banquet God has prepared. I like Luke's expression as he tells this parable: "Go out to the highways and hedges, and *compel* people to come in, that my house may be filled" (Luke 14:23). This passage expresses the eagerness of God to share his goodness with us, the desire of our Father that we should partake of his joy. I shall try to remember these things when uncertainties arise, and they will. For truly he is "a stronghold to the needy . . . a shelter from the storm and a shade from the heat."

A Sure Saying! AUGUST 13

Psalm 51:1-10 and I Timothy 1:12-17

The saying is sure and worthy of full acceptance, that Christ Jesus came into the world to save sinners. And I am the foremost of sinners. I TIM. 1:15

"Worthy of full acceptance." That has two meanings to me. It means that those who do not accept this sure saying miss the greatest blessing they could possibly have. They reject God's answer to their greatest need: the need of forgiveness for their sins. Without that forgiveness, mankind wallows in self-justification, rationalization and a kind of hard, strenuous effort to make oneself "good." But sooner or later we fail to carry through. Then our conscience smites us that we are not "good," and we have to begin the process of self-justification and excusing ourselves all over again. Forgiveness cuts across all that. We can just own up to the fact that we are sinners, that Jesus came to save sinners, and that he forgives every sin that we confess to him in repentance.

There is a second meaning here, too, I think. "Worthy of full acceptance" suggests that we need to accept fully the reality that we are flawed, imperfect, fallen creatures. Paul had no difficulty with that, he just labeled himself "chief of sinners" (King James Version) or "foremost of sinners." In either case, he accepted fully, to the core of his being, that he needed a Savior. In another place he writes, "whatever was gain for me I counted as loss for the sake of Christ." Anything that made him want to boast and take credit, he felt, took away from the glory that he should give to Jesus Christ. "Full acceptance" is a way to relax and receive the mercy of God on the deepest levels of our heart.

In Remembrance of His Mercy AUGUST 14

Isaiah 61:1-4, 8-11 and Luke 1:46B-55

He has helped his servant Israel, in remembrance of his mercy, as he spoke to our fathers, to Abraham and his posterity for ever.
LUKE 1:54-55

We must live, at least in part, in hope of what God will do in the future. It is right that we not borrow trouble from an unknown future, nor live in some kind of unreal dream world. The present is the life we know, and we should not waste it either by worrying or wishing! But (and it is a very big but)—we will inevitably worry about the future or repress our worry and become dead and cynical—unless we have faith in the God who is in our future and who makes and keeps promises. Once we are firmly relying on an unchanging God who "in remembrance of his mercy" orders and arranges our little lives as well as the course of the stars and of nations, we can let go, relax, and begin to see how much there is right here and now to be enjoyed and appreciated.

Mary was sustained by her unshakable faith in God and in her hope of what he would do. "Behold, from henceforth all generations will call me blessed," she sang, even when the generation around her would call her impure. That is hope. And it has come to pass as she sang. We do indeed call her blessed! That is fulfillment.

What about us? Is there anything in our lives that should dim our hope for the morrow? Do we have to face anything—any suffering, trial, pain, circumstances—without the God who remembers his mercy and keeps his promises? Whatever else the birth of Jesus means (and it means far more than we can ever talk about), it also means that God remembers and God fulfills. That is a strong and sure word for us when we begin to doubt, to worry, to think that things are "hopeless." Nonsense! Things are never hopeless as long as God remembers his mercy.

By the Mercies of God   AUGUST 15

Psalm 138 and Romans 12:1-8

I appeal to you, therefore, brethren, by the mercies of God, to present your bodies as a living sacrifice, holy and acceptable to God. . . .   ROMANS 12:1

In today's psalm I find a verse that is very meaningful to me: "Though I walk in the midst of trouble, Thou dost preserve my life" (verse 7). I suspect that many of you who read these words could echo that prayer. We do have to walk in the midst of trouble at times, and sometimes the trouble seems overwhelming. I find that it doesn't take much bodily discomfort or weakness to bring up some unwanted feelings of fear and anxiety, and I have to go back to the throne of grace and offer that fear to God. For I know in very truth what the psalmist is saying here: "Thou dost preserve my life."

In our text from Romans, Paul is appealing to Christians to let go of everything that would keep them from belonging fully to God. But he does not base his appeal on fear. Rather, he bases it on "the mercies of God." God never asks us to do anything without giving us the grace and strength to do it. He is not playing some kind of cruel game with us. And when he asks us to present our bodies "a living sacrifice," he is saying, offer everything you are and everything you have to me. After all, he gave us life, and gives us breath moment by moment. We belong to him, and he is our Creator and Lord. So it is not unreasonable for him to say, "present your bodies a living sacrifice." God knows that when we do that, we are going to experience much more in return than we give. And the evidence is this: the past mercies of God! "Count your many blessings, name them one by one." By remembering his mercies, we draw nearer to the heart of the God of mercy. His mercies endure for ever. So on the basis of those mercies, he asks us to give what we can, not to hold anything back from him, so that we can belong to him fully and receive the fullness of his blessings. "I appeal to you . . . by the mercies of God."

Better Than Life   AUGUST 16

Psalm 63 and John 14:8-17

So I have looked upon thee in the sanctuary, beholding thy
power and glory. Because thy steadfast love is better than life,
my lips will praise thee. So I will bless thee as long as I live.
PSALM 63:2-4

This psalm does not start out with these beautiful words, and the caption at the head of the psalm reads, "A psalm of David, when he was in the wilderness of Judah." Those were hard days for David. On the one hand, he had been anointed to be king of Israel. On the other, Saul, the reigning king, fearful and jealous of David, sought to take his life. "My soul thirsts for thee, my flesh faints for thee, as in a dry and weary land where no water is."

What do we do in such times? Give up and go on about our business? The temptation may be very great to do just that. But the psalmist has a better way. He remembers. "I have looked upon thee in the sanctuary, beholding thy power and glory." The vision of God's love and mercy that was given us in the past was not for that moment alone. It was to sustain us in the time when we have such feelings of dryness and lifelessness. God has not changed just because our feelings have changed! He is still God. His kingdom still rules over all. Have we looked on him in the sanctuary? Have we beheld his glory on the cross—dying for us, giving his life for our life?

The "mountain top" experience is, for most of us, a rare one. Most of life is lived on the lower plane of duty, of struggle, of conflict. There we prove our sincerity in our walk with God, and there we meet with mercies "new every morning." And the memory of such moments when we have caught a glimpse of the majesty, the glory, the victory and the power of this great God can sustain us and enliven us in our "dry and weary land where no water is."

Through the good times and the dry times, we can still say with David. "Because thy steadfast love is better than life, my lips will praise thee; so I will bless thee as long as I live"—in dry seasons and in times of consolation.

Nothing Can Separate Us from the Love of God

Matthew 13:44-50 and Romans 8:26-39

For I am sure that neither death, nor life, nor angels, nor principalities, nor things present, nor things to come, nor powers, nor height, nor depth, nor anything else in all creation, will be able to separate us from the love of God in Christ Jesus our Lord.
ROMANS 8:38, 39

In Romans 8:28, Paul makes the bold assertion that "all things work together for good" to those who love God. If God *is* at work, and all things are by his will or his permission, working together with his overarching Providence for good—then we are safe in going on with Paul to make the statement in today's text. He begins by saying, "I am sure," or "I am persuaded." And we can ask, " How did that happen? How did Paul become so sure of what he is saying?" The answer is clear: he is persuaded by his experience of God's love and mercy. Paul had suffered a lot. But his suffering was never without God's grace.

Can you say the same for your own life? Are you willing to be persuaded that God has been and is now working—or letting things work together—for your good? Although many things in my life have brought pain and suffering, even bewilderment at times, looking back I can make that same statement. "God meant it for good."

Paul's point here is that *nothing* will be able to separate us from God's love. Why? Because God loves us without limit—his is an eternal love. You may not always feel God's love or even be certain of it in your mind, but God is with you, even when you think he has forgotten you. So hold on to the truth. Nothing can destroy the love that has claimed you, the love that will never let you go.

The Interceder   AUGUST 18

Acts 2:1-21 and Romans 8:22-27

*For we do not know how to pray as we ought, but the Spirit
himself intercedes for us with sighs too deep for words. And he
who searches the heart of men knows what is the mind of the
Spirit, because the Spirit intercedes for the saints according to the
will of God.*   ROMANS 8:26B AND 27.

How do we grasp this great truth, that the Spirit of God
within us intercedes on our behalf? The wonderful
thing is that we are not left alone in our weakness and
need—"our infirmities," Paul calls them. One of the titles
given the Holy Spirit is "Paraclete." Jesus says in the John's
Gospel, "I will ask the Father and he will give you another
Helper, to be with you forever. This is the Spirit of truth,
whom the world cannot receive." That word "Helper" is also
translated "Advocate" and "Comforter." Here the Lord
promises that the Spirit will stand with us, and will be with
us to teach and strengthen us at all times—"to be with you
forever."

Today's Scripture also tells the wonderful story of the
first Pentecost, when the Holy Spirit was poured out on the
apostles, and miracles resulted. It was the occasion when
that frightened band of defeated men and women was
changed to people of courage and boldness. Not that they
were never frightened or discouraged, but now they had
within them "the Helper," the Interceder.

Life as we know it has its frightening and troubled times.
There are dark days as well as sunny ones. Sometimes we
"coast along" and are hardly aware of any special needs we
have. We can just enjoy the scenery of life as we journey
through it. But then storms arise. Unexpected news, like a
clap of thunder, disturbs our tranquility. Our health may

deteriorate, loved ones may be having a hard time. Things may get so dark that we think we haven't the ability or courage to carry through as we ought. Then, "in sighs too deep for words," the blessed Spirit intercedes for us. And with his help, we make it through. That is a gift to be cherished, to be praised and to evoke our eternal, unending love.

Grace and Peace   AUGUST 19

Isaiah 45:1-7 and I Thessalonians 1:1-10

Grace to you and peace. I THESSALONIANS 1:1

As I watched on television a small portion of one of the memorial services held for the victims of the TWA 800 tragedy in late July 1996, I was touched by the song they were singing: "Amazing grace! how sweet the sound! that saved a wretch like me. . . . Through many dangers, toils and snares I have already come; 'Tis grace that brought me safe thus far, and grace will lead me home."

What is it that gives this song such a universal appeal? I think that when we face ultimate things, or the most ultimate thing, we become aware of our need at a new level. Those hundreds of people gathered on the Long Island shore certainly were aware that there was a unity in their common need and common grief.

Grace is the undeserved, unearned favor of God. Grace does not depend on our goodness or our good works. Grace is for those who know they are not perfect, that they have failed to live up to the best they know. Grace is for flawed, wounded people—and that is all of us! But grace is *favor.* If you favor someone, that means that your goodwill is toward that person. If you favor someone, that means that you really care what happens to him or her. That is what grace says about God. So when Paul says to the Christians at Thessalonica, "Grace to you," it is both a prayer and an affirmation. God's grace has already been shown to them as they heard and received the gospel of Jesus Christ. They had turned from their old ways. God's grace had already been operating in their lives.

Along with that grace Paul prays for "Peace." We can offer that prayer not only for ourselves but for all those we know. For God's grace makes possible "the peace of God which passes all understanding." Even in the midst of affliction and trouble, we can seek and find that peace. Perhaps more in times of great need than in "good times" that peace becomes a pearl of great price! May it be yours today.

Start with God AUGUST 20

Genesis 1:1-5, Acts 19:1-7 and Mark 1:4-11

In the beginning, God. . . . GENESIS 1:1

When we think about our spiritual life, our faith, what life is all about, when we think about the world, its future, and what our hopes and dreams and fears might be, we might say "Let's start at the very beginning." That's what the Bible does, of course. It doesn't go into all kind of explanations about how the world was created. It leaves that for people to discover. Nor does it try to convince us of how reasonable it is to believe in God. It simply says, "In the beginning, God. . . ."

Our faith is in the God who was before all things. We cannot grasp with our minds what it means that he is eternal, that he is without beginning or end, because for us, everything we know has a beginning and an end, and we inevitably think in those terms. But even though we cannot grasp what the Bible is saying, we can still believe it. We can say with the Church in every age: "I believe in God, the Father Almighty, Maker of heaven and earth."

But the God whom we meet in the first verse of the Bible is not simply a Creator involved in spinning worlds out into infinite space, making suns, solar systems, stars and atoms. This God is moving toward a purpose of love. His creative act was an act of love—permitting other creatures to have their existence. It's pretty wonderful when you think about it!

This God was not content to stop with mountains, oceans, clouds, trees, flowers, fish and animals. It was his purpose to create a race that could love and be loved, with whom he could speak as Friend with friend. It was a wonderful plan, and even the entrance of sin and darkness did not sway him from his purpose. He has an eternal plan to save and restore that which he created for his own loving purpose.

What does that mean to you and me, as we live out our days and go about our ordinary routines of life? It means that we were brought into this world because God loved us. It means that he has never ceased to love us, even at our unloveliest. It means that Jesus Christ was sent, not only to restore the great creation back to his Father, but to touch your life and mine with his love. So every day, if we begin with God, we begin with the One who continues to give us life, and continues to offer to go with us through all the experiences of the day.

So, let's start at the very beginning. God loves you, and longs to bless you. "In the beginning . . . God."

Rock of Ages   AUGUST 21

Isaiah 59:1-2, 15-21 and Mark 10:46-52

Rock of Ages, cleft for me,
    Let me hide myself in Thee;
Let the water and the blood,
    From Thy wounded side which flowed,
Be of sin the double cure,
    Cleanse me from its guilt and power.

Augustus M. Toplady,
1776

W hen my wife and I were visiting England some time ago, we spent a brief time near Glastonbury, in the western county of Somerset. At the hotel we remarked about the rugged, massive rocks that loomed up on each side of the road, and were told about another group of rocks known as the Burrington Coombe. "You might want to look at it," said the manager. "That's where the Rock of Ages is."

That afternoon we took the road to the Coombe. After a gradual descent, we came upon a group of huge, weathered rocks, looming 20-40 feet in the air. Beside the road was an official sign, "The Rock of Ages." It pointed across the road to a great rock with a cleft large enough in its rough front that a person could get into it, as though the rock had been split in two at some distant time in the past. Engraved on it was: "The Rock of Ages. Here the words of the hymn were inspired when the Rev. A. M. Toplady took refuge here during a storm." I had grown up singing that hymn.

As I looked at that "Rock of Ages," the words of the hymn became graphically clear to me. Surely the Lord is our refuge in the storms of life. Some come on suddenly, unexpectedly. Others remain and do not diminish as we would like them.

When all is said and done, and the battles of life are fought, we can do nothing better than to pray as the poet prayed:

> "Nothing in my hand I bring,
> Simply to Thy cross I cling."

The Rock of Ages will not fail us, and we are safe when we hide ourselves in the shelter of God's loving care.

God So Loved   AUGUST 22

Ephesians 2:1-10 and John 3:14-21

God so loved the world that he gave his only Son,
that whoever believes in him should not perish but
have eternal life.   JOHN 3:16

This may very well be the best-known verse in the Bible. We have all had people who loved us and showed it by the way they cared for us—our parents, teachers, friends, family. We were recipients of love, however imperfect it may have been. Sometimes it may have been chastening or correcting. At other times, it may have meant sharing a common sorrow. So we know, at least a little, of what it means to be loved.

Let's apply this to what God says to us here: "God so loved you that he gave. . . ." *Stop!* Do we know what it means to give? To give is to let go of something, to give up control, so that it is in the hand of the receiver. That is what God has done: He has given us the gift of the present life—to use or abuse as we choose. And here he is offering to give us another dimension and quality of life—eternal life—not just long-lasting, everlasting life, but life that breathes the air of eternity, of God's own life.

When God gave his Son, the world rejected and crucified him. But God did not take back the gift. He still offers it to "whoever believes in him." If we reject the gift, we reject the blessings that go with it, but God has given it and will not take it back.

What have we done with that gift? This life we know is being used up day by day, moment by moment. Jesus came to give us life that is life indeed, life that will never be used up. But unless by simple faith we receive him, we'll miss the joy of it. And how do we do that? Simply, as a child receives its Christmas gift or birthday gift with joy. We can just accept what God is offering. There is no trick, no magic, no series of rites or ceremonies that we must go through. God gives. We receive. The Gift is ours.

Our Help and Hope   AUGUST 23

Psalm 90 and I Thessalonians 2:1-8

Lord, thou hast been our dwelling place in all generations. . . . So teach us to number our days that we may get a heart of wisdom.
PSALM 90:1 AND 12

The psalmist is contemplating what life and aging mean. He thinks of God's age. "Before the mountains were brought forth, or ever thou hadst formed the earth and the world, from everlasting to everlasting thou art God." In another place God is referred to as the Ancient of Days. God has been around a long time (so to speak) and he knows very well what is going on. He also knows what we need in our short lives. He knows far better than we do what we need to prepare us for the blessings he has in store for those who love him.

Thinking about that preparation, the psalmist prays, "So teach us to number our days that we may get a heart of wisdom." Since we know that our time on earth is limited, we should pray that same prayer: "That we may get a heart of wisdom." Let us pray to make wise choices in the present circumstance of our lives. Here are two suggestions:

(1) Pray that bitterness and resentment will be removed from your heart. Forgive those who have wronged or hurt you at any time, and ask God's mercy on them.

(2) Pray that your love for Jesus Christ may dispel your fear of the future. If we know that the Lord is with us, surely we will be able to face the future, for his love is greater than any trial we may experience.

May the Lord enlighten your heart in this part of your journey through life, and give you great peace of mind as you grow in faith and hope.

The Best Love   AUGUST 24

Luke 4:21-30 and I Corinthians 13:1-13

So faith, hope, love abide, these three; but the greatest of these is love. I CORINTHIANS 13:13

We are greatly affected by what we love. Paul is talking to the Christians at Corinth about the love they have received from God through their faith in Jesus Christ. He describes it in rather careful detail in this 13th chapter of I Corinthians. It is the kind of love that caused God to send his Son to be our Savior, and to love us in spite of all our unloveableness. Maybe you have had people who loved you "in spite of who you were." I know I have!

What are some of these other loves that affect our lives? There are both noble and ignoble kinds, honorable and dishonorable. There is self-love, a sick, inordinate concern about *me*. It's the kind of "love" that is apt to manifest itself when we are hurting, or when we are afraid that we are going to be asked to suffer more than we can stand. It's the kind of love that demands, demands, demands.

Then there is the love of *things*. All too many of us know what that kind of love can do—it can drive us to cling even to small things as though they gave meaning to our lives. It can make us unwilling to share what we have with others. Not a nice kind of love, really.

Then there is love of family and friends. That's good—a noble kind of love, if it does not insist on being the *most* important thing in our lives. Even family and friends cannot be God, and God is jealous of his rightful place in our hearts. So even the best human love can be a danger if it is not submitted to the greater love of God.

God Will Take Care of You AUGUST 25

Romans 10:5-13 and Matthew 14:22-36

Jesus immediately reached out his hand and caught him,
saying to him, "O man of little faith, why did you doubt?"
MATTHEW 14:31

> Be not dismayed, whate'er betide,
> God will take care of you.
> Beneath his wings of love abide,
> God will take care of you.

The words of this hymn have to be understood in the right way, for God doesn't give us everything we want just because we want it. He *is* taking care of us like a loving Father, and that means that he always reserves the right to say "No" if what we ask would be harmful to us.

But the theme of the song—and the theme of today's Scriptures—is most certainly true. God *will* take care of you, and is *at this very moment* taking care of you. You may be experiencing some kind of limitation on your former freedom, whether you are in a hospital, a nursing home, a prison, or perhaps just in the familiar surroundings of home. In such circumstances, we may be tempted to feel that life is too hard, too unbending. The temptation is always to go into a dark dungeon of self-pity and despair. And we may be afraid of things getting worse!

Jesus' kind word to Peter after taking his hand and keeping him from sinking into the sea is a good word to you and me: "O man of little faith, why did you doubt?"

Recalling the many times when his loving hand has come to our aid will help us to banish present doubts. Remembering to recall and *give thanks* for the many blessings he has given us will be even more helpful in dispelling our doubts and gloom. What the hymn and the Gospel are saying is this: You are dear to God. He loves and cares, and he takes care of you because of that love. You can be at peace within yourself because that is true. God *will* take care of you!

God: The Beginning and the End   August 26

Acts 5:27-32, Revelation 1:4-8 and John 20:19-31

"I am the Alpha and the Omega," says the Lord God, "who is and was and who is to come, the Almighty." Revelation 1:8

In modern language, we might hear God saying, "I am the A and the Z—the first and last, the beginning and the end." That is what our text is saying. So what is the message for us? Let's think about it together.

We came from God. Before we were, before anyone else was, even before this beautiful, weary world was—God is. We know that intellectually, but what does it mean practically? It means that our life is a gift from him who is Life itself. He has allowed us to experience life here on earth for this short span of years. I say "short span," for no matter whether our years are 80 or 100, they are still short compared with God's eternity!

In giving us life, God has given us minds to think with. We have been able to learn many wonderful things. A very dear friend of ours used to say, "Learn something beautiful every day." When she died at the age of 86, she was literally in the process of memorizing one of the Psalms. She tried to learn something beautiful every day. Any of us could do that if we chose. It would be a good use for our minds. St. Paul said, "Whatever things are true, whatever is lovely, whatever is gracious . . . think on these things." There is so much ugliness that offers itself to our minds—resentment, anger, self-pity, jealousy, stubbornness—that we must guard against giving in to it. Instead, we can choose to think on better things, and in doing so, become better people.

In that gift of life, God has given us hearts to feel with. And today's text says he is the beginning of everything and the end of everything. That means that love—his love—gives us life, sees us through life, and meets us at the end of life. What more could we ask of him than that?

Today, his love is right here with you and me. Let us embrace it, rejoice in it, find hope and courage in it, and let us be channels of it to all who meet us. And that will be enough!

Strength and Bright Hope   AUGUST 27

Psalm 145 and Romans 7:21-8:6

For to set the mind on the flesh is death, but to set the mind on the Spirit is life and peace.   ROMANS 8:6

The Lord is good to all and his compassion is over all that he has made.   PSALM 145:9

Today's psalm and New Testament lesson encourage us and lift our heart above our circumstances and surroundings. It is always possible to become discouraged or disheartened by keeping our eyes fixed on things around us. There may be circumstances in our lives that are distinctly unwelcome and unpleasant. Or the future may be so uncertain as to cause anxious thoughts to rise unbidden when we are least prepared to fight against them. We have all experienced their intrusion, too.

Paul reminds us that if we insist on setting our minds on the flesh (that is, on all that is apart from God, being concerned simply for this world, our own desires, etc.), we experience death. There is no life in things of the flesh. I think we could all say we have found that to be true. We just end up in a blue funk, hopeless and at a "dead end." But, he says, if we set our minds on the Spirit, we experience life and peace. There is a way out of the mental and emotional pit if we choose it. Jesus Christ has provided the way.

> Pardon for sin and a peace that endureth,
>> Thy own dear presence to cheer and to guide;
> Strength for today and bright hope for Tomorrow,
>> Blessings all mine, with ten thousand beside!
>> *T.O. Chisholm*

There is strength for today's needs and bright hope for tomorrow because God's mercies really and truly never come to an end. His mercy is here with me as I write, and is there with you as you read. Adequate strength for whatever you face. And a bright hope for whatever future lies ahead.

But we must choose to set our minds on the Spirit instead of on ourselves if we would know that this is the way to life and peace. And it is possible to do so because God loves you and because Jesus Christ gave his life to bring us this peace and hope.

For Which Food Do You Labor? AUGUST 28

Exodus 16:2-4, 9-15 and John 6:24-35

Do not labor for the food which perishes, but the food which endures to eternal life, which the Son of man will give to you.
JOHN 6:27

A few years ago I had a very devastating experience. I was driving along in my car, praying about something which was bothering me. Then, in the quietness and privacy of my car, I had something like a revelation. It was a shocking realization that everything (as far as I could recall) I had done which I thought was good was somehow mixed with wrong motives. I had wanted to be praised and well thought of, or had wanted to "get ahead" in my profession, or had wanted my family to make me feel good by being the way I thought they should be.

But that moment did bring me face to face with an important question: what do I really want out of life—the "food which perishes," or that which endures to eternal life? And then I knew that deep in my heart I wanted the latter.

Life has a funny way of putting us in circumstances where we can get a different perspective on things and reappraise what life is all about. I've known this to happen to people who were temporarily or permanently disabled, or who faced a difficult situation they could not change or control. In such a circumstance, we have a choice. Jesus says, "Do not labor for the food which perishes." In other words, "Don't live your life for that which just passes away with the using. You were made for better than that!"

The Israelites in the wilderness fretted and worried (as we do) because they couldn't be sure they would have sufficient means to live to get to their journey's end. I've known older people who really worried for fear their money would run out before they did—and failed to enjoy what God had given them. So God showed Israel that he could rain down bread from heaven to keep them going.

Jesus says that he is the true Bread from heaven. We can lay down our worry about what people think of us or how they treat us, our resentment because things don't go the way we would like. And we can seek daily to be fed inwardly from the secret Source, "the peace of God which passes all understanding." We can let today's circumstances, which we cannot change, become the time to choose to live for eternity.

Wonderful Words of Life AUGUST 29

Jeremiah 15: 15-21 and Matthew 16:21-27

Thy words were found, and I ate them, and Thy words became to me a joy and the delight of my heart; for I am called by Thy name, O Lord, God of hosts. JEREMIAH 15:16

Jeremiah was one of the greatest of the Old Testament prophets. His was a weighty and unpopular task—to prophesy the downfall of the nation before the judgment of the Lord. But before he was ready for that job, he first "found" God's words—he made himself acquainted with God's thoughts and God's will. To do so was not easy for him, because God's will was quite different from his own. But as he discovered God's words, they became the joy and delight of his heart. He still had the unpleasant task of preaching a very unpopular message to an unwilling people, as today's Scripture makes clear. But God assures him that he will be with him in his difficulty and will redeem him from the grasp of the ruthless.

As I read over that lesson, I thought of how we take for granted that we have Bibles available to us all the time. It has not always been so. People have suffered imprisonment, torture, and even death in order to be able to hear, read and know God's word. There was such life in it for them, such hope was kindled by it, so brightly did it inflame their faith that they were willing to undergo much for the sake of God's Word, which had become a joy and the delight of their heart.

But what of us? The only way we can find out the treasures of God's Word is by acquainting ourselves with it. To do so may not be easy—certainly not as easy as turning on the television set—but it is much more rewarding. The Bible speaks after all of the real issues of life—your needs, our sins, God's love, Christ's salvation, our hope for time and eternity. These words really are "wonderful words of life." A daily discipline of reading quietly a short selection of Scripture can bring a new sense of order and peace to us. If you are not already doing this, why not begin today? A good place to start is in one of the Gospels. You need not read a lot, but prayerfully, thoughtfully (in a kind of conversation with God) let the words speak to your heart and your condition.

The Oil of Gladness AUGUST 30

Isaiah 61:1-4, 8-11 and I Thessalonians 5:16-24

The Spirit of the Lord God is upon me, because the Lord has anointed me to bring good tidings to the afflicted. . . . to give them a garland instead of ashes, the oil of gladness instead of mourning. ISAIAH 61:1A AND 3B

I have been having trouble at times recently experiencing "the oil of gladness." Recovering from two major operations, my spirits were at times so low I was really ashamed of myself. "What am I doing in this state?" I asked myself. "I have ministered God's truth to others for many years. And now, in my dark hour, I find myself fearful and consumed with self concern."

I think I've always looked for a "quick fix." If I prayed for something, I would look for a quick answer. If it didn't come, I would begin to doubt whether prayer was even doing any good, and often times would just quit praying about the matter.

The prophet says that the Spirit of the Lord has anointed him to give those who mourn the oil of gladness. Someone has said that the Lord is always on time, never late. When these dark hours come and stubbornly remain, it is our task and our privilege to keep on praying. "This kind does not go forth except by prayer." We have a weapon for warfare here, and I think in my case, God is calling me to learn to use that weapon more faithfully, more consistently.

In the hospital before surgery, I confided to an assistant who came into my room that I was experiencing anxiety. She looked at me and said, "But you know where your strength is!" I felt rebuked and encouraged at the same time. She added, "Through all the years, he has never failed me yet. I will pray for you." And I'm sure she did. I saw again the tremendous power of prayer and the privilege of praying. Paul's word in today's Scripture is: "Rejoice always, pray constantly, give thanks in all circumstances." Let the dark hours enlarge the scope of your prayers. Pray not only for yourself and your need to have peace in your heart, but pray for others who are also facing the valley of the shadow.

Aiming High AUGUST 31

I Corinthians 12:12-31A and Luke 4:14-21

But earnestly desire the higher gifts. I CORINTHIANS 12:31A

Paul is talking to young Christians—not necessarily young in years, but young in the faith. They have been converted from one or another of the pagan faiths which were numerous in that first-century world. And one of the things that attracted them to Christianity was the evidence of the reality of God. "Spiritual gifts" were a sign that people were not just talking about God, but that they were dealing with a living, caring God.

But Paul sees a problem here—and that is "latching" on to such unusual displays and making them primary. Apparently some of the people were jealous of others who seemed to have more important or impressive spiritual gifts. So Paul speaks an important word to all of us: aim at the highest gifts. In the next chapter, he will discuss the highest gift of all—but now he seems to be counseling us to "aim higher."

It is not a distortion of the spirit of this text to apply it to our situation. If our day is occupied with the most limited concerns, we may miss the greater blessing that is there for the taking. If all we are concerned about is "how I feel," "what I want" and "why is this happening to me," such "low" concerns can deafen us to the music of the heart, or blind us to the vision of God's great mercy. The old Shaker song said, "Tis a gift to be simple, a gift to be free, a gift to come round where we ought to be." Life is a gift. Today is a gift. Learning to appreciate it, to have gladness in our heart and thanksgiving to the Giver—these are gifts not to be despised.

So, today, whatever may be our aches and pains or the limitations with which we have to live, let us "aim higher," and accept his best gifts!

Follow Me

"Come follow me," Jesus said,
"and I will make you fishers of
men." At once they left their
nets and followed him.

MATTHEW 4:19-20 (NIV)

Grampy's Wave

I remember the beach at Red River
you swam and floated with us
between the jetties
took long walks in the sand
you were always friends
with the lifeguards

Those were the early years
of doughnuts
from Bonatts
on Saturdays
and riding Big Wheels
in the driveway

In later years
you would work
on the garden tomatoes
while we sent badminton birdies
to nest permanently
in the branches
of backyard trees
you made our breakfast
and poured the juice
the last time we met for breakfast
your hands shook,
so I poured instead
long swims
had turned into drives
the garden had vanished
we watched Red River

from the car
you stood at the door
and waved good-bye as we left—
the walk to the end of the drive
was too long

when I looked back,
the twinkle in your eye
and your smile remained
your hand circled round
in that funny wave
that only we could understand

that's how I'll remember you
Grampy
standing in the doorway
waving us
good-bye

Paige Cleverly

Come to Me

Psalm 91 and Matthew 11:25-30

Come to me, all who labor and are heavy-laden, and I will give
you rest. Take my yoke upon you, and learn from me; for I am
gentle and lowly in heart, and you will find rest for your souls.
MATTHEW 11:28, 29

It is a sad thing that we see ourselves only in terms of the work we do. What is so much more important is what we are. And I think a lot of us do not yet know as fully as we ought what we are, or who we are. So when we get to the point (temporarily or more permanently) when we can no longer do the work we once did, we feel useless, like so many "cast-offs."

Now Jesus understood just what we are like inside. He knew that our labor is not only physical work. There is another kind of inner labor, of burden-bearing which may go along with our physical work, and wear us out far more than we ever experienced from our jobs. It's the kind of inner uncertainty and turmoil that comes from living apart from God. True freedom, true rest, true liberty come by taking his yoke upon ourselves. Taking his yoke upon us means seeing ourselves in our heart of hearts as his followers, his disciples, yes, his friends. That's what he invites us to be, as he says, "Learn from me, and you will find rest for your souls."

The struggles of life can be exciting. The challenge of work can call for the best we can give. But the time comes to lay down the tools—for a day, a week, a month—or longer. There is a time for learning more deeply that the true meaning and true reward of life comes not from what we have done or failed to do, but from a living, loving relationship with our Lord. That's what he was talking about in today's text. "Come to Me . . . and I will give you rest."

The Faithful Shepherd

SEPTEMBER 2

Psalm 80:1-11 and I Corinthians 1:4-9

*Give ear, O Shepherd of Israel . . . Stir up thy might
and come to save us.*   PSALM 80:1A, 2B

*God is faithful, by whom you were called into the fellowship of
his Son, Jesus Christ our Lord.*   I CORINTHIANS 1:9

Have you noticed how honest the Psalmist is when he
talks to God? Sometimes he almost sounds irreverent.
His need is so great and his faith in God is so strong that
he doesn't hesitate to cry, "Make haste . . . stir up your
might . . . why do you sleep? . . . have you forgotten us?"

I think we'd get a lot farther in our relationship with the
Lord if we learned to be more honest with him. Too many of
us want to hide our sins, even when we are aware of them,
tuck them away out of sight, hoping no one will notice.

And wouldn't the relationship between us and others be
a lot more peaceful and a lot more pleasant if everyone was
quick to acknowledge when our feelings were hurt, or when
we'd said something we were sorry for, or when we realized
we'd hurt someone else? Trying to pretend an incident didn't
happen is simply storing up trouble for the future—and if we
do that long enough, there will be a real barrier between the
persons involved. Perhaps no cross words will be spoken,
but the barrier, the separation, will definitely be there.

And so it is with the Lord. Unless we can cry out our
needs from the depths of our heart, we'll be convinced he
doesn't really understand or care. Our relationship with him
will suffer from our lack of honesty.

Paul knew all about that. He had prayed earnestly—and
still didn't get what he was praying for—the removal of his
"thorn in the flesh." But that didn't destroy his confidence in

God, because he received something from God better than he asked for—the assurance that God's grace was sufficient for him and that God's strength would be perfected in Paul's weakness. God blessed not only Paul with that assurance, but millions of others who have read those blessed words.

And out of such experiences Paul could write, "God is faithful." What more do we need in order to face whatever life is giving us at this moment? God is faithful—he is the Good Shepherd who knows us by name, who leads us along right paths—and who will safely fold us with his own flock. Such faithfulness demands that we, too, seek to be faithful to him—faith full—full of faith, trust and thanksgiving.

The News Is Still Good   SEPTEMBER 3

Isaiah 40:28-31 and Luke 4:14-21

The Spirit of the Lord is upon me because he has anointed me to preach good news to the poor. LUKE 4:18

Jesus went back to Nazareth (where he had been brought up) and in faithful fashion, went to the synagogue on the Sabbath day. He was about to begin his ministry that would forever change the world, and there was no better place to do so than in his home town.

It was apparently the custom that any rabbi was free to speak at the sabbath service. In the rural South, where I grew up, a visiting preacher was given the same courtesy. And so Jesus opened the Book to Isaiah where the prophet spoke of the Promised One. Jesus read the words of today's text: "The Spirit of the Lord is upon me, because he has anointed me to preach good news to the poor." After a few more sentences, he said, "Today this scripture has been fulfilled in our hearing."

Jesus came with Good News. His mission, his purpose, his object in life, he said, was not to be served but to serve. He came to seek and save that which was lost. He came as a physician to heal the sick. He came as a Herald to announce that God's kingdom had drawn near.

What did all this mean? That people were to look up from their bondage and hear words that would free them from fear. That they were to give up their slavery to anger, jealousy, greed and self-pity, because God's love was being offered them in a new and saving way.

He still offers the same Good News to us. He sets the captive free; he gives sight to the blind. And he puts a new song in the heart of those who accept his Good News. May that song brighten this day and all your days.

Abraham's Sacrifice and Ours   SEPTEMBER 4

Genesis 22:1-14 and Matthew 10:40-42

After these things God tested Abraham. . . . Now I know that you fear God, seeing you have not withheld your son, your only son, from me. GENESIS 22:1 AND 12

The heart cries out, "What is being asked here? And why would God ask such a thing of any parent?" In Abraham's case, he had already been put to the test by having to wait years and years for Isaac in response to God's promise to give him an heir. The Bible says that Abraham was a hundred years old when Isaac came. Abraham's hope was tied up in this child. And yet God asked him to give him up.

I remember stories I have read about mothers and fathers whose son or sons were killed in battle. They were asked by their country to "give up" their child for the country's sake, and most of them carry their grief with dignity and pride. So we know that it is possible to surrender even a child of our flesh and blood to a higher goal or purpose.

But I also think of other things that God asks of us—testing us, if you will, to see if we are as sincere in our love for him as we like to think. Right now, I suspect, you may be facing this question on some level. Has he asked you to give up some of your freedom, or is it your belief that life should be pain-free and care-free? Is he asking you to believe in him in spite of your fear and worry about the future—to put your life in his hands in a greater degree?

We say "yes," but we begin to grumble about our circumstances, we doubt that God is really in charge, and we may begin even to question whether God loves us and cares about where we are. Abraham showed that he preferred God over all. If we hold on to anything in this life that God is asking us to turn over to him, it robs us of the peace and joy he wants us to have.

At the end of the story, the place of sacrifice was called "The Lord will provide." He never shortchanges his children, and always gives us back more than he asks us to give to him.

Worthy of the Gospel — SEPTEMBER 5

Philippians 1:21-27 and Matthew 20:1-16

Only let your manner of life be worthy of the gospel of Christ, so that . . . I may hear of you that you stand firm in one spirit.
PHILIPPIANS 1:27A

The people of Israel had every inducement to live up to God's standards for them. Yet they failed to do it. They were cautioned over and over to repent and let their lives conform to his ways, but the Old Testament is a sad account of repeated failures on their part.

Moses was on the mountain receiving the divine law when the people turned to idolatry and revelry. How quickly they had forgotten! They thought only of today, and Moses was gone. Old attitudes and old ways came back quickly.

Paul knows that we all share the same human nature. We want to change, but old patterns are hard to break, and the well-worn ruts are there to slip easily into. So Paul encourages us with this counsel: "Let your manner of life be worthy of the gospel."

What kind of person are you? Do you radiate cheerfulness, courage, confidence in God? Or do you express fear and frustration, fretting over little things day by day? It is important to bathe your spirit in the light of God's love, his many mercies, his abiding grace. In this way, no matter what period of life you are in, you can "let your manner of life be worthy of the gospel of Christ."

Do Not Be Afraid . . . SEPTEMBER 6
for He Has Risen!

Psalm 118:14-24 and Matthew 28:1-10

But the angels said to the women, "Do not be afraid; for I know that you seek Jesus who was crucified. He is not here, for he has risen, as he said." MATTHEW 28:5, 6A

The fear of death is a common human experience. From early childhood we come to know that death somehow threatens our continued existence as we know it. And although we push away the thought of death, refuse to think about it, or think of it only when we have to, it is still there—a threat that hangs over all we are and all our relationships. Apart from its threat to us personally, it threatens to separate us from those we love.

We come to the Easter story in the four Gospels after having been given detailed accounts of Jesus' last days—the suffering, pain, humiliation and injustice he experienced. Throughout those Gospels, he reminded his disciples that this would happen to him, and assured them that "after three days" he would rise again. But they, like us, were not prepared to take him seriously.

Such a thing was too good to be true, they thought. But, oh, it was true! It is true! Jesus really did come out of the tomb, leaving behind his burial cloth, appearing and talking with the disciples for forty days, so that they would not think they had simply seen a vision or had dreamed it up.

All of this was to give us the assurance we need that this life is not the whole story, that we are destined for something so far beyond our imagination that we cannot conceive it! In his great love for us God has opened the gate of eternal life. We can live knowing that death does not have the last word!

In our life we, too, have to face suffering and hardship. We have to face temporary separation from those "we have loved long since and lost awhile." But we can have daily fellowship with the living Lord; we can live in the calm assurance that he will be with us throughout and beyond this earthly life. This is what Easter proclaims.

Foolishness or Wisdom? SEPTEMBER 7

Exodus 20:1-17 and I Corinthians 1:18-25

*For the word of the cross is folly to those who are perishing, but
to us who are being saved, it is the power of God.*
I CORINTHIANS 1:18

Folly. That's what the world called it when those early Christians went out across the world saying that Jesus Christ had died on the cross so that people might return to God and have new life.

Folly. That's what the religious leaders called it, who thought that the only way to be right with God was to behave correctly.

Folly. That's what the world still calls it. To the worldly mind, a Christian is a mysterious being who does not swim with the current of the multitude.

Years ago, my seminary professor said that people would say to him, "I don't need all this Christian religious stuff. The Ten Commandments and the Sermon on the Mount are enough for me." And he would reply, "Well, they're too much for me, and that's why I need the Cross."

What did he mean? When he read the Ten Commandments and the Sermon on the Mount, he realized how far short he was falling from what God intended. When that realization comes, there is only one answer: forgiveness. When we face ourselves honestly, we can receive God's pardon and peace, with humility and gratitude.

The power of God. That's what Paul called "The preaching of the Cross." It had transformed him from a hard, self-righteous Pharisee into a loving, compassionate soul. And that's what literally millions of other Christians have found in the centuries since.

The power of God. This is such a simple word we may overlook it. It says that we do not have to live in vain regret and remorse, nor do we have to pretend we are better than we are. "The word of the cross . . . to us who are being saved . . . is the power of God."

With Jesus on the Way   SEPTEMBER 8

I Peter 1:17-23 and Luke 24:13-35

While they were talking and discussing together, Jesus himself drew near and went with them. But their eyes were kept from recognizing him.   LUKE 24:15, 16

Those two unnamed disciples are really a picture of all of us. We walk along life's road, talking together about things that disturb us, things that delight us, things that fill us with questions or wonder. We are grateful for human companionship by which we can share the truly important things of life. Most of us, however, do not readily talk about the things that matter most. We worry and fret about little things, and most of us have no difficulty in expressing these small concerns. But we have a much harder time talking about the deeper, more important issues—our fears about the future, our resentments about the way life has turned out for us, our questions about dying, and so on. Yet we would fare much better if we spoke openly of these things to someone we can trust.

The disciples in our Scripture today had no trouble talking about the things that mattered most. Jesus had been crucified, and they had been so frightened, shocked and grieved by all that had gone on that they had not known what to do. Then that very Sunday morning, reports had begun to come to them that Jesus had been seen alive and that some of the people who went to his tomb had seen angels.

Now a Stranger drew near and began to talk with them. He entered into their discussions, began to open up their understanding about God's plan, and showed them that everything that had happened all fitted into what God had long beforehand foretold through the prophets. Their hearts burned with new hope and quickened faith. They wanted the Stranger to stay with them longer, to talk more, for surely "he had the words of eternal life." And so they prevailed upon him to tarry. When he took the bread and broke it, suddenly they recognized that it was Jesus himself who was with them.

Dear friend, whoever you are, that same Jesus is with you. You may be totally unaware of his presence, but he is there, loving you, blessing you, wanting to give you his blessing. All we need is to have our "eyes opened" to see his gracious hand, leading, healing, comforting, correcting us.

Being Glad for God's Love SEPTEMBER 9

Psalm 31 and John 14:1-14

*I will rejoice and be glad for thy steadfast love,
because thou hast seen my affliction, thou hast taken
heed of my adversities.* PSALM 31:7

I find as I grow older I love the Psalms more. There is such honesty with God there—no playing around with simply pious words, but honest, real conversations with the Lord. The psalmists knew what they were talking about and they knew the Lord to whom they spoke.

In today's psalm, in his great need David is crying out to God. And so we have a kind of "back and forth" between his distress and his full confidence in God. In verse 9 he cries, "Be gracious to me, O Lord, for I am in distress, my eye is wasted from grief, my soul and my body also." Yet just a few lines earlier he has said, "I will rejoice and be glad for thy steadfast love." In other words, David could not keep himself always in a positive, cheerful, hopeful frame of mind, because he was a human being with changing feelings, and his problems were very real ones.

I remember an incident from many years ago when one of our children was very small. His mother and I took turns staying with him in the hospital as he received painful, frightening shots of penicillin around the clock. As I sat there through the long night hours, I found myself asking over and over again, "Why? Why does this have to be?" By God's mercy, our son recovered and is now a healthy adult, and is himself a minister of the gospel. But the agony of those hours is still etched in my memory. It was a time when I tried to be utterly honest with God. What this psalm is teaching us is that we do not honor God by hiding our true feelings from him, and that our deepest needs are not shocking or strange to him. Since he knows us, and accepts us, we can come to him in full confident faith that he will hear and help us in our need. It is even more true of us, who have the full revelation of God's love and mercy in Jesus Christ, for grace in our time of need!

And They Were All Amazed   SEPTEMBER 10

Deuteronomy 18:15-20 and Mark 1:21-28

And they were all amazed, so that they questioned among themselves, saying, "What is this? A new teaching!" MARK 1:27A

I suppose people will never get over being surprised—"amazed"—at Jesus. One of the most popular hymns of all time is John Newton's "Amazing Grace." What is it that we find so amazing about Jesus, that generation after generation reacts just like that first one?

First, his amazing kindness. From the beginning, Jesus talked about little children, widows, and the poor and needy. He talked with women—even the Samaritan woman by the well; he befriended prostitutes and set them on their way to a new life and new self-respect. He touched the lepers, the blind and the deaf. All these people, so looked-down upon by society in general, Jesus loved. He showed them kindness, compassion, mercy. And people were "amazed."

Second, his amazing authority. There is nothing in the Gospels to suggest that Jesus was a pale, "meek and mild," pastel Jesus. He was vigorous and strong, and knew how to take command. He had authority in his teachings that astounded those who heard him. They were used to the kind of teaching that relied on scholarly knowledge, quoting the authorities "from old times." But when Jesus spoke, he sounded as though he had just come from the presence of his Heavenly Father, and had received his message directly from him. It was fresh, direct, to the point. And people recognized the authority within him as he spoke.

And he had authority over diseases and demons. Whether the sickness was emotional or physical, or a combination of both, he spoke the word that freed people into new wholeness.

Finally, there is his amazing sacrifice. It would have been remarkable enough if he had simply preached the Good News, called people to a new way of life, healed the sick and cast out the dark demons of despair. But his real mission was to bring the human family back into reconciliation with God. The problem goes to the core of humankind. It lies in the heart. And here he made his most amazing act of grace: he laid down his life for us. For somehow the cross touches us at the core, convicting us of our selfishness and rebellion. It speaks tenderly of forgiveness offered. And because the story does not end there, it promises us the power and life we need to become different on the inside.

We stand amazed in the presence of Jesus . . . and love him, because he first loved us.

But God Loved Us   SEPTEMBER 11

I John 4:7-12 and John 15:1-8

In this is love, not that we loved God but that he loved us and sent his Son to be the expiation for our sins. I JOHN 4:10

This little section of John's first letter is one of the most simple and profound statements in the Bible. Here we have those unforgettable words, "God is love." You can say that God is powerful, almighty, omnipotent, but the Bible never says "God is power." You can say that God is all-knowing, omniscient, wise beyond our thoughts, but the Bible never says "God is wisdom" or "God is knowledge." But as the Apostle seeks to convey what he and the others have learned from their years with Jesus, he sums it up in those beautiful words, "God is love."

But that word "love" is a tricky one, because people have used it in so many wrong ways that we have to be careful how we use it. We say, "I just love that movie." "I love ice cream," or a thousand other things.

So how do we find out what love really is? Our text says that we do not find it in our good feelings about God, but in the reality of what God has done for us. He shows his love for us in Jesus Christ—his life, his teachings, his suffering and his death. "In this is love, not that we loved him, but that he loved us." If we want to see the height, breadth and depth of true love, we look to Jesus.

Love is costly. You cannot love people without caring about what happens to them. If they hurt, you hurt with and for them. If they sin, you grieve for them. Is this not what we see in Jesus? He told the story of the shepherd who had one sheep who went astray. So great was his love that he left the ninety-nine others and went after that one. This is a picture of how much God loves us, and to what lengths he goes to bring his wandering sheep home. It is a costly love that knows no limits.

In our honest moments, we have to confess that we do not love as God does. Our love is weak, self-oriented and unstable. We need more of his love to replace our human, imperfect love. Let us pray for more of his love, for our love can be perfected only in his.

Founded on the Rock SEPTEMBER 12

Genesis 12:1-9 and Matthew 7:21-29

Every one then who hears these words of mine and does them will be like a wise man who built his house upon the rock.
MATTHEW 7:24

Today's Gospel reading warns us that it is not enough to say "Lord, Lord." Jesus warns us that God is God and that we must take seriously what he has told us if we want to enter his Kingdom. This is not a negative thing, though. because God reveals himself to us as more merciful and gracious than any of us could ever imagine him to be.

We are building the house of our souls day by day. Is that house on the firm foundation of faith in Jesus Christ and a desire to belong to him? If it is to stand in the storms, it cannot rest on our own morality, our honesty, our truthfulness or our decency. Paul says in I Corinthians 3:11, "No other foundation can anyone lay than that which is laid, which is Jesus Christ." He will stand when all else fails.

> How firm a foundation, ye saints of the Lord
> Is laid for your faith in his excellent Word.
> What more can he say than to you he hath said,
> To you who for refuge to Jesus have fled?

The day of testing comes for everyone, says Jesus. Circumstances grow difficult, sickness or other misfortunes befall us. What we do then depends on the kind of foundation we have built. It does not depend on our being able in ourselves, for no one is so strong that circumstances cannot weaken us.

The time comes when all human help fails—no matter how well-meaning it may be. Then we have the blessed assurance, if we are trusting in the Rock of our salvation, that he will not fail!

So let us turn to Jesus anew in these quiet moments and give him permission to be the everlasting Foundation of our lives. Whether this is our first time to do so, or whether we have done so many times, we need to let him know and let ourselves know that we are, right now, putting our trust in him.

> On Christ, the Solid Rock I stand!
> All other ground is sinking sand.

Take Heart, It Is I!   SEPTEMBER 13

Romans 9:1-5 and Matthew 14:22-33

But immediately he spoke to them, saying, "Take heart,
it is I; have no fear."   MATTHEW 14:27

The image of life as a "wild, surging sea," and our own place in it as being in a small boat, is surely a familiar one. Here we see the germ of the image: the disciples in a boat, Jesus apart from them about his Father's business, a sudden unfavorable wind preventing them from rowing to safety.

Does that story sound familiar? Does it describe any experience you have ever had, when you felt yourself struggling against seemingly impossible circumstances, unable to make them any better? I suspect that in such a case, all of us are tempted to feel that the Lord is far away—not in the middle of the trouble with us!

But this is where Jesus comes walking across the water—symbolically entering the most impossible of our circumstances in his own way! His comings and goings are not like ours, and are always fitted to what is best for us. So if we are in need of comfort and reassurance, we can be very sure that he will come. We may have to wait (for very good reasons that we may not yet understand), but come he will, and nothing can keep him out.

We get into trouble by believing that he is not able to help us, that he is not Lord of the situation we face. That attitude leaves us feeling orphaned and open to all kinds of bitterness and self-pity. As people of faith, who have already had many experiences of the providence and mercy of God, we can fight against these self-generated feelings of fear and resentment and assure ourselves that God is good. "I will recount the mercies of the Lord," says the psalmist. We may be literally overwhelmed for the moment by our unhappy circumstances. But remember, the psalmist says, "All *thy* waves and billows have gone over me" (Ps. 42:7). Whatever the circumstance, it is God's circumstance—by his will or by his permission—and he is never absent from us as we are called to go through it.

That is why Jesus can say to the disciples, "Take heart, it is I." We, too, can take heart, because he is here with us now, however we may feel, whatever our need may be, however wide and stormy the sea of life may seem at the moment. There is mercy and goodness and an opportunity for a deepening of faith and a softening of the heart hidden in every unfavorable circumstance. The eye of faith will see it and rejoice.

Help My Unbelief! SEPTEMBER 14

Isaiah 50:4-9 and Mark 9:14-29

And Jesus said to him, "If you can! All things are possible to him who believes." Immediately the father of the child cried out and said, "I believe; help my unbelief!" MARK 9:23, 24

Recently I attended the funeral of a fellow minister, a friend of many years, who had died after a sudden, massive heart attack. One of the greatest things said about him was that he was completely honest with God. It was said of him that he pleaded with God, begged God, demanded of God that he change him from what he was to what he knew God wanted him to be. "Lord, I love you a little; make me love you more. Lord, I believe in you a little; help me believe in you more." So his testimony was not one of great achievements but of persistent determination to be God's man. Now that is something everyone of us can aspire to, and we can pray with all our hearts like the father of this stricken child in the Gospel: "Lord, I believe! Help my unbelief!"

Jesus challenged that man to believe when it was hard to believe. After all, the disciples had tried to help the child and had failed. Then Jesus came down from the Mount where he had been transfigured before Peter, James and John. Seeing the problem, Jesus began to inquire about the child's condition, and the father answered, "If you can do anything, have pity on us and help us." Jesus' answer pushes the gate of heaven ajar a little. "If you can! All things are possible to him who believes."

Most of us have never dared accept that challenge. It seems too good. Or, like children, we may have taken it as license to make God into our heavenly Santa Claus, only to be disappointed when he doesn't play our game. But Jesus is calling for a faith that dares, a faith that is willing to ask for a miracle. And the greatest miracle is the change within that makes us what God wants us to be. The greatest achievement in life is to come into harmony with God, to be at peace with God with whom we will live for all eternity. All other things fade into insignificance beside that achievement. I challenge you to believe when believing is hard, and pray as my friend did, "Lord, I believe in you a little. Help me believe in you more!"

Why Are You Cast Down?   SEPTEMBER 15

Psalm 43 and Matthew 23:1-12

Why are you cast down, O my soul, and why are you disquieted within me? Hope in God; for I shall again praise him, my help and my God.   PSALM 43:5

The words of this text appear three times in Psalms 42 and 43. Perhaps the psalmist was feeling a little sorry for himself. We all know what self-pity and discouragement can do if we allow it to gain the upper hand. It can so distort our thinking that we begin to feel hopeless, and think life has treated us very badly.

In the beginning of this 43rd Psalm, the writer asks God to vindicate him before the enemy who is oppressing him and seems to have gained the upper hand. Now, our enemies are not people who are trying to conquer us, or people who make fun of us. You remember that there were those who railed at Jesus when he hung on the cross, saying, "If you are the Son of God, come down from the cross" (Matthew 27:40). It wasn't enough that they had succeeded in getting Jesus crucified. They had to relish their triumph by reviling and mocking him. So whatever we feel of discouragement, we can be sure that Jesus has tasted circumstances far, far worse than any we have to brave.

Nevertheless, we do have a spiritual enemy, the adversary of our souls. And the conditions we face sometimes give our enemy the opportunity to harass us. Thoughts and feelings come into our minds that make us doubt that God knows or cares where we are. We may not recognize this, but at that very moment, we are in a spiritual battle. The psalmist recognized this, and gives us a way of fighting against discouragement.

First, ask yourself why you are cast down. Think about it. Tell God where you hurt and what makes you feel sad. He is always more ready to hear than we are to pray.

Second, talk to yourself as the psalmist does. He says, "Hope in God! I shall again praise him who is my help and my God." These feelings will pass. They are not permanent, and they can be dispelled if we use the weapon God has given us. Praise him. Thank him. Bless him. Remember his past mercies. Tell him that you know he is your help and your God. Try it. I believe you'll find it helps.

When Did We See Thee? SEPTEMBER 16

Psalm 123 and Matthew 25:31-46

And the King will answer them, "Truly I say to you, as you did it to one of the least of these my brethren, you did it to me."
MATTHEW 25:40

Recently I was admitted to the hospital for major surgery. Before I went, however, I was admonished in these words: "Look for love in everything that happens. Look for love in the people and in the circumstances." And in the days that followed, those words kept coming back to me as I did indeed experience love in countless ways.

When we look for love we are really looking for God. I found in the hospital that the doctors, nurses, and workers were bearers of God's love to me. One lady from Trinidad came into the room every day to perform a certain chore. But with her came a radiant cheerfulness that brightened the whole room. Even outside the door, you could hear her cheerful voice and infectious laughter. Who can measure what a word of cheer or of encouragement can mean to those who come into our lives day by day?

I thought of that experience as I read today's Gospel. As spoken by our Lord, the emphasis is on how we treat others, how we respond to their needs. You may feel that you don't have much opportunity to respond to other people's needs at this point. But I suspect that if we look around us with the idea of sharing love with others, we will find many, many opportunities to do so.

Jesus is saying in this parable that he is coming to us in many different ways. He is giving us the opportunity to serve him as we serve one another.

Today, if you choose, you can be a messenger of God's love. And you can be a recipient of it. Look for love. Look for him in your present circumstances. He is there for you.

Temptations and Testings   SEPTEMBER 17

Romans 5:12-19 and Matthew 4:1-11

Then Jesus was led up by the Spirit into the wilderness
to be tempted by the devil. MATTHEW 4:1

The first thing that strikes me about this text is this: it tells us that Jesus was led by the Holy Spirit into the desert to be tempted. Now we know that God does not tempt anyone. "Let no one say when he is tempted, 'I am tempted by God'; for God cannot be tempted with evil and he himself tempts no one" (James 1:13). So what does this mean? I believe it means that this was a testing time that the Spirit was leading Jesus to accept.

Temptation and testing are very closely related. Jesus was the perfect man, offering perfect obedience to the Father as no human being has ever done since the fall in the Garden of Eden. This testing in the desert is symbolic of the entire life of our Lord, in which he in every respect has been tempted as we are, yet without sin (Hebrews 4:15). At every turn Jesus chose the Father's will. He passed the test. He met temptation but did not give in to it.

Jesus faced many tests, and the greatest one was, of course, when he faced the Cross. You and I face many tests, and I think the greatest ones are the things we cannot control—our health, our future, our circumstance.

These are testing places, and Jesus not only shows us how to meet them, but he actually is here with us to help us make the right choices. A cousin of mine with a serious heart condition lives alone. After a brief visit with her recently, my wife remarked, "The thing that impressed me most about your cousin is that there is not a smidgen of self-pity in her. She does not feel sorry for herself and does not try to make others feel sorry for her. That's a good demonstration of her faith in God!"

I want to make the right choices when testing comes, so that when it is over, I can hear the Lord say, "Well done, good and faithful servant." Don't you?

Finding Heart-Rest   SEPTEMBER 18

Philippians 4:1-9 and Matthew 22:1-14

Have no anxiety about anything, but in everything by prayer and supplication with thanksgiving let your requests be made known to God. And the peace of God . . . will keep your hearts. . . .
PHILIPPIANS 4:6 AND 7B

There it is again: a call to lay aside our anxieties and worries. Does it seem like an impossible request? Most of our anxieties are so imperious, so demanding that they pretend to be inevitable. "Now, if you have any sense, you'll know that you ought to worry about this," they seem to say. And sadly, we too often believe them and fall prey to their lie.

Why is anxiety a lie? Because it accuses God of being unable or unwilling to be with us in whatever it is we fear. Think about it: is your anxiety not always about what "might happen" in the future? Mine certainly is.

Every day brings us new opportunities to trust God and to live in the awesome reality of his love. Every day we can, if we choose, look for and find his hand in what is happening in us and around us.

I can't think of any gift that would be more valuable to any of us than "heart rest." To be at peace with oneself, with God, and with one's lot in life—this would be a gift beyond telling. For no matter how much wealth, property or achievements we might have, if we do not have this heart rest, we are poor indeed. And this is what the Lord offers his children. "Come unto me, all who are heavily burdened, and I will give you rest." It's heart rest that he is talking about. So when Paul tells us, "Have no anxiety about anything," he goes on to tell us how to make our requests known to God. We are to pray for what we need or what we desire "with thanksgiving" for what we have.

Recently I remarked that my left wrist was not "happy." It had been giving me pain for a couple of days. My good wife replied, "Then give thanks for all the joints of your body that are happy!" I knew she spoke a truth I needed to hear: not to concentrate on what was wrong, but to give thanks for all that is right. So I'm doing that, even as I write these words. I hope that they will help you to find the peace of God and the heart rest I knew he wants to give you.

Take Up the Cross   SEPTEMBER 19

Psalm 24, Philippians 2:5-11 and Matthew 16:21-28

If any man would come after me, he must deny himself and take up his cross and follow me.   MATTHEW 16:24B

There are three words in this text that really hit home: deny, cross, and follow. For in our nature there is nothing that wants to be denied. We want what we want when we want it. That's all of us. And God lovingly says, "If you want to be like me, if you want to be like Jesus in your heart," deny that self that demands what it wants when it wants it. Say no to it!

The second word—cross. For a long time the cross was

a beautiful symbol of what God did for me. As far as my cross was concerned, I thought it was made of those self-denials I willingly chose to take on. Then a wise teacher one day was talking, and she said, "The cross is whatever cross-es me out." As she said it, she made a motion of a cross coming down from her head to her waist, and from shoulder to shoulder. That gesture turned on lights for me, for there are lots of things in our lives that "cross us out" and give us what we would not choose to have. And Jesus said, ". . . take up your cross." Don't be angry and try to avoid that which is "crossing you out," but let it make something very freeing and good happen inside.

Follow me. We do want to be more like Jesus, don't we? We want to be where he is—for there is light, joy and life. Darkness dwells where there is sin, fear and despair. So if we want to be "his followers" we can say "Yes" to him and all he wants to bring into our lives. Doing so will lower us in our own eyes, but we will find it the way of life, joy and peace.

Entreat Me Not to Leave Thee   SEPTEMBER 20

Psalm 146 and Ruth 1:1-19A

. . . Entreat me not to leave you or to return from following you; for where you go I will go, and where you lodge I will lodge; your people shall be my people and your God my God.
RUTH 1:16

For us, the meaning of this text cannot be limited to its original context. Somehow the words leap out and demand to speak to situations far removed from that of Ruth and Naomi. For they are words of the heart, and, although spoken in a specific situation, they transcend it. To me, they are the words of the faithful soul spoken to our Lord and Savior Jesus Christ.

First of all, think of all that would "entreat" us to leave him. There is the obvious fact that we have no external proof that following him will bring the blessing we need and seek. Ours is, and must be, a faith walk. That means that sometimes the clouds of doubt, the darkness of the unknown, the bitterness of grief or loss, the anxiety of sickness—all crowd in to suggest that believing and following are not worth it all. So we have these temptations to think it isn't worthwhile to believe and follow Christ.

Second, there are the weaknesses and failures on our part that accuse us and suggest that we are wasting our time. Who has tried to walk the path of faith and not been smitten with his or her own failures or shortcomings? The nasty temper which seems unconquerable; the temptation to say ugly things about others; the times we have given in to self-pity, fear, anxiety, jealousy. Sometimes we get to feeling that there's no use trying, because we're bound to fail. But, come back to our text.

Ruth's spirit was expressed by her decision to follow. It was not only Naomi who had captivated her heart and loyalty. "Your God shall be my God," was the way she put it. Tennyson has one of his characters say to the king, "There is something in your countenance I fain would call Master." Can we not say the same for our Lord? There is something in his look, his life, and his death that grips us and makes us want to call him Master, Lord. And so to him we can say, no matter what our circumstances may be at this moment— "Entreat me not to leave you, or return from following you. For where you go, I will go. Where you lodge, I will lodge, and your people shall be my people, and your God shall be my God."

Bowing the Knee SEPTEMBER 21

Philippians 2:5-11 and Luke 19:28-40

Therefore God has highly exalted him and bestowed on him the name which is above every name, that at the name of Jesus every knee should bow. . . . PHILIPPIANS 2:9, 10A.

The way to glory for Jesus was through humiliation, degradation, pain and death. It involved laying down his life and all that was dear to him—save only his love for God and his obedience to the Father. All earthly ties had to be loosened and let go. Are we surprised that he calls us to walk the same path that he walked? Is it strange that we, too, must lay aside our claims on everything that ties us to this earth, so that God might be all in all?

Paul reminds us that in this act Jesus was completing his life of obedience. "He became obedient, unto death. . . ." That is all the way. Whatever he had felt or desired, he had put aside in order to fulfill his Father's will. And that says something to all of us who call ourselves "Christians." Our call is not only to believe, to say "Hosanna" at the right time, and to wave our palms in the air, our call is to follow him in our obedience.

Sometimes obedience gets downright inconvenient. Sometimes it involves letting others have their way when we want very desperately to have ours. Sometimes it means accepting pain and discomfort when we long to be free of it. Sometimes it means dealing with our faithless fears and accepting God's will as better than our own. Obedience can be costly, because we are not by nature obedient people. We are independent and rebellious. So obedience comes of struggle and hard decisions. But if we believe in him, if we love him, if we desire to be like him and to be with him, his word to us is a simple one: "He who loses his life for my sake shall find it." And that word is sealed with his own life's blood.

Day by day we are given a chance to love and honor our King. For most of us, we will show that love and reverence by the attitudes we take towards our life, the circumstances we cannot change, the people we live with, the things we must do, or the things we cannot do. If in our hearts we choose to let the circumstances whittle away the overgrowth of self-love and self-concern, then we are loving and honoring Jesus. If we choose to become rigid and bitter, feeling that we are victims of unfairness, that life should have treated us better, we are turning our backs on Jesus and his cross.

The Power of the Cross   SEPTEMBER 22

I Corinthians 1:10-17 and Matthew 4:12-23

For Christ did not send me to baptize but to preach the gospel, and not with eloquent wisdom, lest the cross of Christ be emptied of its power.   I CORINTHIANS 1:17

Both of today's readings mention "preaching." In Matthew's Gospel we are told that Jesus went preaching, "Repent, for the Kingdom of God is at hand." That was the same theme that John the Baptist had preached when he appeared on the scene.

Jesus came to announce the coming of God's kingdom, God's rule among men. He said over and over again that the kingdom was "at hand." The apostles were told to go out and preach the same message, for people were not ready for God's rule. A radical change was needed to get them ready for the new Day.

But as the disciples put their trust in Jesus who had died and risen again, they found their lives changed. Repentance became a reality, and they could face all the problems of life with new strength and hope. Not that they were always brave, strong and true! Far from it. They were like us, and sometimes they stumbled as they went along, but there was no disputing that a new Day had dawned for them. From that time till now, millions of sincere folk have entered into this new life of forgiveness, faith and hope. The Kingdom of God has drawn near.

Paul preached this simple truth and people accepted it, and the "power of the cross" still works miracles in lives of those who believe. I commend it to all of you who read these words. Look to him and let him work that wonderful change in your life that will turn you from darkness to life, from doubt to faith, from bitterness to hope.

Good Tidings to the Afflicted   SEPTEMBER 23

Isaiah 61:1-11 and I Thessalonians 5:16-24

The Spirit of the Lord is upon me, because the Lord has anointed me to bring good tidings to the afflicted. ISAIAH 61:1A

It is remarkable how much of the Bible is concerned with people who are having a hard time. The whole history of Israel in the Old Testament is an account of their struggles with their "neighbors" and within themselves. They continually went from one trouble to another, and the Lord continued to teach and lead them toward his promised goal.

When Jesus stood up in the synagogue to preach his first sermon, he chose this text: "The Spirit of the Lord is upon me, because the Lord has anointed me to bring good tidings to the afflicted." That the Son of God should announce his mission in those terms should certainly be a continual source of encouragement and comfort to us "in all our affliction."

How can we best let those gracious words do their work in us?

First, try to face your own "afflictions" honestly. To deny that we feel them is not the best way to confront them.

Second, choose to believe that God is for you instead of against you. The present circumstances are either by his will or by his permission. In either case, he plans to use those circumstances to bless you. You can choose to believe that.

Third, wait on the Lord, expectantly, persistently, until he is able to break through and flood you with his blessed peace that passes understanding. Keep asking, seeking and knocking until you experience what he wants to give you. There is good news for all our afflictions!

Think on These Things   SEPTEMBER 24

Psalm 135:1-14 and Philippians 4:1-9

Finally brethren, whatever is true, whatever is honorable,
whatever is just, . . . pure, . . . lovely, . . . gracious . . .
think on these things.   PHILIPPIANS 4:8

What do you think about? What fills your thoughts? Do you think this is a foolish and unimportant question?

Actually, what we think about is one of the most important things that should concern us. Too many of us allow our minds to be filled with things that drag us down instead of lift us up. We allow our thoughts to be dragged down to the lowest level instead of lifting them up to the Lord.

An old Puritan maxim said, "Plain living and high

thinking." "High thinking" points us to the same things Paul urges upon the Philippian Christians—to fill our minds with whatever things are true, honorable, just, pure, lovely and gracious.

Along that line, I'd like to share a recent experience. A dear friend of ours died recently, and as she lay in the hospital realizing that she was dying, she said something to this effect: "The things that have meant so much to me mean nothing to me now. They are all useless, worthless." She was close enough to eternity to know that many of her priorities had been wrong.

I wonder how many of us need to face the fact that we have entertained altogether too many burdens of self-pity, anger, resentment, hurt feelings, jealousies, fear and doubt—when we could just as easily have cast them away, and by the grace and forgiveness of God in Jesus Christ, we could have chosen to fill our minds with love, joy, peace, forgiveness, reconciliation, contentment, graciousness towards others. Paul calls these "the fruit" or "the harvest" of the Holy Spirit, which every believer has dwelling within us. So we are not victims of these dark thoughts. We can choose to think on the higher things, seek the higher things, and find the higher way.

That Your Joy May Be Full   SEPTEMBER 25

Psalm 98 and John 15:9-17

*These things I have spoken to you, that my joy may be in you,
and that your joy may be full.*   JOHN 15:11

If it were not possible for us to have joy in Christ, he would
never have told us these things. If it were not possible for
us to fight feelings of sadness and hopelessness, God would
not have asked it of us.

We believe in and serve a good God. He has planned
good for us, he wills good for us, and he works around us
and in us to accomplish his good will. That is the condition
of our life—whether we recognize it or not.

In our life of faith, God seeks to bring us to fullness of
joy. That joy comes out of a trusting, abiding relationship
with him. If we are in harmony with him, we can take the
changes and chances of everyday life without despair. We
can say, "Father, I trust you, even if I cannot understand this.
I choose joy instead of grief. I choose to align my heart with
yours. Let your joy be my safeguard."

It is not always easy to choose joy. Sometimes I find it
easier just to feel a little sorry for myself. The pains and
aches loom large, and I wish that life might be the way I
imagine it should be. The main thing is, when we find ourselves "down," and feeling a little or a lot discouraged, to let
our feelings press us to the Lord of Joy, who "for the joy that
was set before him, endured the cross, making light of the
shame." There *is* a joy to be found. There is a secret peace
for those who seek it. There is an answer to our prayers.
Finding it and accepting it is part of the excitement of
belonging to him. May his joy fill your heart today!

To Do or to Endure   SEPTEMBER 26

Acts 2:37-41 and John 16:5-15

When the Spirit of truth comes, he will guide you. . . .
JOHN 16:13A

In the Gospel text, Jesus is talking to his disciples about what the Holy Spirit would do in their lives after he, Jesus, had gone back to heaven. The Spirit is sent to convince us of where we are wrong and the need to change. (Read John 16:8.) But the Holy Spirit does not come to make us feel guilty, because he also offers us the forgiveness of God as soon as we see where we are wrong. A lot of us carry around a low-level feeling of fear or anxiety, because we have not wanted to even consider where we might be (or might have been) wrong. In that case, we bring guilt upon ourselves, but that is not God's doing. The Holy Spirit pricks our hearts and conscience—where we have been cross, demanding, ungrateful, jealous, fearful—and then he bids us confess that wrong to God so that we might be free from its evil effect. It is a wonderful and encouraging thing that we have the Holy Spirit right inside us to correct and heal us where we have missed the mark.

The Spirit is also sent to guide us into all truth. What a tall order that is! Think of all the different ideas bounding around in the world, claiming our allegiance, claiming to be "the Truth." What are we to think? How are we to choose? Thank God, we have been given a Helper, the Spirit of Truth. If we turn our hearts toward him and desire his will above our own, we can trust that the Spirit within us will help us find and know his truth. We can depend on these as a guide for sorting out conflicting ideas, and we can ask the Spirit to show us whatever truth he has for us.

There is another thought about the Holy Spirit that I want to share with you. In one hymn we pray that God's Breath (the Holy Spirit) will be so breathed into us that our wills and his will can become united as one. That's what it means to have a pure heart—to choose the same thing God chooses—no mixture of loyalty. We do this or choose to endure whatever God sends; our wills and God's will become more united.

Sometimes we see that there is less to do and more to endure, and doing is easier than enduring. But we have come a long way with God, and if he is calling on us to endure some difficult situation, he will not leave us to endure it alone. We can count on that, and by the inner strength of his presence within, we can choose to endure.

The Marvel of Unbelief   SEPTEMBER 27

II Corinthians 12:1-10 and Mark 6:1-6

And he marveled because of their unbelief.   MARK 6:6A

The Gospel takes us back to Jesus' home town of Nazareth where he had grown up. He had returned from a wonderful mission. Great crowds had thronged to him, he had cast out demons, he had helped and healed many people. But now he was back among those who had known him as a child and as a young man, who knew his mother and his family. And they chose to look at him with critical eyes. They could not believe that one who had come from among them could do such things as were being reported. In spite of all the testimonies, in spite of all the evidence that God was working wonders through him, they would not believe.

And Mark says of Jesus, "He marveled because of their

unbelief." It seemed to him very strange that in the face of so wonderful a thing, they chose not to believe. The sad thing was that their unbelief actually blocked the working of the Holy Spirit in their midst. Unbelief is resistance to God. It is not neutral. It is a stubborn refusal to come under the supernatural authority and power of our Creator. Unbelief insists on having the last word, making everything understandable or calling it unacceptable.

But we do not have to stay locked in unbelief. We can begin to doubt our doubts. We can choose to believe that God is greater than we have imagined. We can pray, "Lord, I believe; help my unbelief!" We can choose to lay hold on his promises by faith, and we can begin to experience something new and wonderful in our relationship with him. Faith can grow; doubt can fade. Life can replace death. Light can replace darkness.

Choose today to believe in him: believe in who he is, in his mighty power, greater than our needs. Open yourself to the inflow of God's power to quicken, renew and enliven you within.

God Is Faithful   SEPTEMBER 28

I Corinthians 1:3-9 and Mark 13:32-37

God is faithful, by whom you were called into the fellowship of his Son, Jesus Christ our Lord.   I CORINTHIANS 1:9

The older we get, the more reason we have to agree with what St. Paul is saying here in this text. This letter was written to Christians living in one of the most corrupt cities of the Roman Empire in the first century. They were surrounded by every kind of sin and evil, and yet, in his great mercy, God had touched their hearts and called them to a life of faith and holiness.

This text is very relevant to you and me, no matter what our age or condition. Life is truly an unfolding of his faithfulness to us, and even in those things that we count tragedies, sorrows, or great difficulties—yes, even in those things his faithfulness is demonstrated.

Recently I have been reading a book by Elisabeth Elliot, *A Path Through Suffering*. You may remember that in 1953 she and her husband, Jim Elliot, were missionaries seeking to carry the gospel to the Auca Indians in Ecuador. The Aucas were a primitive people who had not been reached with the gospel, and in an attempt to make friendly contact with them, Jim Elliot was killed along with four other young missionaries. Not only did Elisabeth Elliot stay on and continue the mission work for another six years (the Aucas were reached and many of them became Christians), but Elisabeth went on to write and teach, reaching literally millions of people with her accounts of the faithfulness of God. Writing years later about the tragedy and loss, she says, "Here was a new chance to choose happiness and peace. They were not something that merely happened to be because I was lucky. . . .They were given in proportion as I chose to see my sorrow in the light of the transitory [the merely passing] and the invisible [that which is eternal]." That is true for us all, in losses and sufferings of every kind. We can choose what we will do with it, and that choice makes all the difference!

Willing to be Convinced?   SEPTEMBER 29

I Timothy 6:11-19 and Luke 16:19-31

[Jesus] said to him: "If they do not hear Moses and the prophets, neither will they be convinced if someone should rise from the dead." LUKE 16:31

Some people need a lot of convincing before they choose to commit themselves to God. They keep wanting "proof" that he exists. They want others to assure them that it is all right to believe. Jesus came into the world making no claims for himself, but offering evidence that he truly is the Promised One, the Messiah foretold by the prophets, the Son of God. He referred to himself by that somewhat mysterious title, "Son of Man," but he did not hesitate to announce that he had come to inaugurate a new age, the Kingdom of God. The essence of his message was, "The Kingdom of God is near; repent and believe the Good News." He wanted people to know that God was doing a new thing, making a new breakthrough into human life.

But faith still has to be a matter of choice. It is not enough to live in a country that has a Christian heritage, where Christianity has always been part of its life. It is not even enough to live among Christian people, or to be a member of the church. Our faith must be an inward matter of the heart. Jesus said in today's Gospel that there is enough evidence to convince any fair-minded person of the truth of what he preached. If a person is an honest seeker after God, there is evidence enough to stand on. "How firm a foundation is laid for your faith!" If we choose not to believe, no one will stop us. Nothing can convince the person who chooses to remain the skeptic and does not wish to be convinced.

Thanks be to God, when we choose to put our trust in

Jesus Christ, his reality is there. His Spirit witnesses to our inner spirit that we are beloved children, and we find new strength and hope beyond our petty weaknesses. Recently, someone wrote, "We still have our problems, but 17 years ago we invited Jesus into our lives, and that has made all the difference." That's good news!

Our Reasonable Sacrifice   SEPTEMBER 30

Romans 12:1-8 and Matthew 16:21-27

I appeal to you therefore, brethren, by the mercies of God,
to present your bodies as a living sacrifice, holy and
acceptable to God, which is your spiritual worship.
ROMANS 12:1

We all know something about sacrifice, since there are people we love. We know that to sacrifice for the good of some loved one is as natural as breathing. So there is a foundation of human experience on which Paul is building here.

The basis of our sacrifice is our love and gratitude. Upon this foundation we can choose to forego what we might prefer, preferring instead the good of the one or ones we love.

Paul bases his appeal to the Christians at Rome on these same two foundations: love and gratitude. He calls us to sacrifice, not to appease an angry God, or to make up for something we have done, but in response to what God has already done for us. On the cross Jesus Christ became the one, all-sufficient sacrifice for the sins of the whole world. That is the accomplished deed, and God is the author of it. We do not have to make sacrifices in order to be forgiven. We have only to repent of our sin and turn to him in faith. But there is a place for sacrifice on our part. Paul says, "I beseech you by the mercies of God."

Because God has provided everything we need for an abundant life here and the hope of eternal life, we can do nothing less than respond to him with all we are and can be. It is a living sacrifice that we are called to be. Just as the Old Testament offering was placed on the altar and offered to God, so we should present our total selves to God as a living offering. Nothing less makes sense.

OCTOBER

Choose Life

*See, I set before you today life
and prosperity, death and
destruction. For I command
you today to love the Lord
your God, to walk in his ways,
and to keep his commands,
decrees and laws; then you
will live and increase, and
the Lord your God will bless
you in the land you are
entering to possess.*

DEUTERONOMY 30:15-16 (NIV)

Freddie

Morning broke refreshingly clear and crisp, more like October than the end of May. The bright sun dispelled the clouds that had hung over us for the past three days, and now as we entered through the cemetery gate, the residual coolness of the night was fleeing, too.

I had conducted well over one hundred committal services, but it was very different to be doing it for my own Mother. Mom had died suddenly, without apparent warning. Very peacefully she had slumped over her typewriter. With a little sigh, she was gone.

We were all glad for her. But the adjustment for us was pretty rough—no known preparation time, no last words to "complete" a dear relationship, no assurance of what arrangements would please her. Besides it was a Memorial Day weekend, an awkward time for any funeral arrangements.

The day before, my dad, my brother and I had come to the cemetery to select a plot. Without saying anything to each other, we had all expected to know instantly which one was right, but we didn't. We had been shown several and had finally selected one, but we left, unsure and disappointed.

That night I had shared with Dad what the brief committal service would be like. He had a lot of difficulty with some of the wording. We wanted to agree, but our overloaded emotions fueled the tension. So it was after an awkward discussion that we finally agreed on what I would do.

Thus, I arrived at the cemetery unsettled inside. I wanted very much to do the right thing for the family and to be God's person in the situation, but I was too involved to be sure I could do that. Besides, I didn't want to break down in the service, and I had no guarantee that I wouldn't.

Our little family group approached our new plot under an apple tree, somewhat secluded by bushes from the noises of the cemetery. Things seemed better than the day before. The service went well, it seemed to me. I didn't stumble over words or get choked up. With the benediction it was over, but in the awkward moment of silence that followed, it became obvious that the words spoken wouldn't be what was remembered of the service.

My dad and I have been avid bird watchers for almost forty years. It took a commitment in our family not to be interested in birds. My mother had made that commitment. But she had one special bird that we always associated with her. Mom had named him "Freddie."

Freddie was a chipping sparrow. He's not a rare bird, but he's not the common sparrow either. He's a cute little fellow with a chestnut cap and a black and white eye stripe. We all had to agree that he did look like a Freddie. For at least twenty-five springs, Mom had triumphantly announced to the family that Freddie was back. We'd all run to the back window and there he would be, poking around in the grass under the swing. He was Mom's contribution to our yearly list.

Dad broke the silence of that moment at the new grave with a quiet "Look!" and as we followed his finger, we all gave a little gasp. There sat Freddie, full of life, on the next tombstone, just as if he were a member of the family. Thirty seconds later he was gone.

We stood there with tears running down our faces, in wonder and gratitude.

God has amazing and very precious ways to let us know that he loves us and that he is with us when we need him most. Freddie became God's benediction on that service, and somehow we all knew that God was confirming to us that Mom was just fine. We also knew that we had picked exactly the right place.

Ronald Minor

Seeds, Soil, and Harvest   OCTOBER 1

Isaiah 55:1-13 and Matthew 13:1-9, 18-23

A sower went out to sow. And as he sowed, some seeds fell along the path . . . on rocky ground . . . upon thorns . . . on good soil.
MATTHEW 13:3-8

The point of the parable of the sower seems to be that the seed, which stands for the Word of the Kingdom (Matthew 13:19) was the same in every case. There the similarity ended. The soil on which the seed fell and the ultimate outcome were totally different.

As I read this lesson over again, it struck me (for the first time, I think) that at different times all of these soils have been pictures of my own life. Sometimes I have heard the Word without understanding, and it was immediately snatched away and bore no fruit. I think of the times which I have been told something I did not want to hear about myself, and instead of taking it as a word from God, just dismissed it and forgot about it.

Then I know that many times I have made good resolutions and resolves, because I had heard something that moved me. But then, the resolution would demand that I give up something or some opinion that was dear to me, and I would just let the resolve die.

At other times, the cares, worries, "responsibilities" and routines of daily life have all but crowded out any serious thought of God's Kingdom (meaning God's will) in my life. But I am thankful that through grace, at times I have heard, understood, and made some response, resulting in a harvest quite beyond my hope or expectation. Perhaps you have had similar experiences.

Right now, at this point in our lives, we have choices to

make. We can listen to God's Word coming to us through the Bible, through others, through circumstances—and choose to receive it and cherish it. His Word grows, we know not how, but it makes inner changes in our hearts. It brings greater peace. It brings more hope. It brings a greater capacity to love and forgive. These are fruits which we can all hope to harvest.

Not As Man Sees   OCTOBER 2

I Samuel 16:1-13 and Ephesians 5:8-14

For the Lord sees not as man sees; man looks on the outward appearance, but the Lord looks on the heart.   I SAMUEL 16:7B

Spoken centuries and centuries ago, those words are as true today as they were then. Human beings (men and women) still tend to look on the outward appearance, do we not? How many times we may have been fooled into thinking people to be something, only to find out on closer acquaintance that they did not measure up to our expectations!

So it is very reassuring to know that whatever the outward appearance may be, God sees the heart. At the same time it is a healthy warning to us, a sober reminder that we are not fooling God. No matter how polite, well-behaved, proper and correct we may be with our outward behavior, it is the heart, the real affection, that God sees.

We may, for instance, carry grudges in our hearts for years, feeling that we are completely justified in our feelings, perhaps not even remembering the incident upon which the grudge is based, but still not letting it go. And so with many things that can clog up our relationships with others, and even more important, our relationship with God. It is an inner heart attitude that matters.

"Man looks on the outward appearance." That may be true of circumstances as well as physical appearance. Circumstances are another "outward appearance." They are the outside conditions, not the heart where we really live. I have known people who were outwardly blessed with wealth, favorable conditions, and physical health, but who were inwardly miserable. And I have known people whose outer circumstances were full of trouble, inconvenience, poverty or uncertainty, yet who maintained a courageous, even sunny attitude through it.

"God looks on the heart." How wonderful that he sees where we cannot see, and he dwells where he can bring peace, hope and joy. The inner man: you can meet the Lord there and find a haven of rest and fulfillment. Seek him.

Thanksgiving and Peace   OCTOBER 3

Philippians 4:4-9 and John 6:25-35

. . . With thanksgiving let your requests be made known to God. And the peace of God which passes all understanding will keep your hearts and minds in Christ Jesus.   PHILIPPIANS 4:6B, 7

It struck me, as I was reading this passage, that there is a very close, vital connection between the thankful heart and the peaceful heart. All of us want the latter, but we do not always take care to nurture the former.

I think, too, how easy it is to lose the spirit of thankfulness. It takes such a small thing to draw our attention away from the many blessings we are receiving, to the one or two small irritations or inconveniences we may be undergoing.

Of course, some of you who read this are being asked to undergo great inconveniences, perhaps even a large measure of suffering. It seems, though, that when God asks us to walk through such valleys of shadows, that there is always a special measure of grace to enable us to endure.

An illustration I read years ago has stuck with me. An honest, outspoken parishioner is talking about what the vicar says in his sermons. She says something like this: "Oh, it's well enough, what he says about dying, and about grieving, and about all those great things. For goodness knows that when they come, you handle them somehow. But 'the price of eggs, Mr. Jones, the price of eggs!' In other words, it was not the great issues, the great trials that muddied up her life, but the little annoyances, like the price of eggs, that she fretted over.

So let us remember that the small things of every day must not be allowed to cloud out the great things God has done for us. Let us give thanks for wonderful sights and sounds to enjoy, for comforts and conveniences that many, many millions of people would consider luxuries beyond their imaginations. And above all, let us give thanks for God's love revealed in our Lord Jesus Christ.

The peaceful heart comes from the thankful heart. May it be yours.

When Others Are More Gifted OCTOBER 4

I Corinthians 12:1-11 and John 2:1-11

All these are inspired by one and the same Spirit, who apportions to each one individually, as he wills. I CORINTHIANS 12:11

There is not one of us who does not know people who are more talented and gifted than we are. Life has not dealt us an equal number of talents and gifts. Even our very personalities are different, and some seem easy to love, some harder.

If we allow ourselves to brood and worry about the fairness or unfairness of it all, we will heap a lot of trouble on our own heads and give ourselves a lot of unnecessary misery. A healthy person is a person who has learned to live with his or her limitations.

This does not mean that we should be content to be vegetables. There are things that we can do something about, no matter where we are. And we must learn to rejoice in the gifts God has given others. They are not given simply for the sake of the person, but to be enjoyed and to be a blessing to others.

In the meantime, Paul reminds us, there are gifts of faith, wisdom, understanding, healing—even the working of miracles—given to various members of the body of Christ. You can be a worker of miracles yourself as you allow the love of God and the spirit of Jesus to fill you more and more. It truly is a miracle to see someone transformed inwardly, even partially. And through faithful prayer—what wonders yet wait to be worked! So why should we ever waste our time, and God's, thinking that it isn't fair that others have so much more than we do. Think rather of how much you have, how greatly you are loved, how many things should cause praise and joy and thanksgiving to well up in your heart. To do so will make all the difference in your day—for yourself and for others.

"It is the same and only Holy Spirit who gives all these gifts and powers, deciding which each one should have." (Living Bible) And after all, he does know best, doesn't he?

Yes, All Things   OCTOBER 5

Romans 8:26-30 and Matthew 13:44-52

And we know that all things work together for good to those who love God. . . .   ROMANS 8:28 (KJV)

This is one of the greatest verses in the Bible. Yet it is one that we probably have the hardest time believing! It is the rare Christian indeed who can say in every circumstance, "I know that this, too, is going to work for good together with everything else." It may be easy to say this in the bright, sunny days when everything is going well. But it is in the twilight, the shadows, the uncertain and difficult times that we need to say it—and mean it.

Writing these little meditations gives me occasion to reflect on how the Scriptures have worked out in my own life. There are glaring examples of the truth of this verse which I missed, or at best, gave only lip service to at the time things were happening.

For instance, I think how God used a most horrible experience in the life of one of my children to bring him "to his senses" when his life was out of control. I would have moved heaven and earth to prevent the circumstance from happening as it did, but looking back, I can see, and with gratitude say, "All things work together for good."

Can you do the same in your own life about things that happened in the past? If we cling to our resistance against what happened, we can miss the blessing God intends. If we stay bitter about something, we are refusing this gracious insight into God's mercy. There is no doubt about it, that the pain we are allowed to experience does a work in our hearts: it deepens and strengthens our faith if we allow it.

Everyone of us is another "unit of confirmation" of the truth Paul expresses here. We are each adding to the story of God's faithfulness to his people as we go through this sinful and fallen world. It is a world of suffering, of broken dreams and unfulfilled hopes. But in it all he is patiently, persistently "working for good" in every circumstance, and he has not forgotten you and me. He loves us and cares deeply about where we are, and we can, by his grace, choose to believe that "all things work together for good to those who love God."

A Heart of Wisdom   OCTOBER 6

Psalm 90 and Matthew 25:14-30

So teach us to number our days that we may get a heart of wisdom. . . . Satisfy us in the morning with Thy steadfast love, that we may rejoice and be glad all our days. PSALM 90:12, 14

The title at the head of the Psalm says, "A Prayer of Moses, the man of God." Someone has said of this psalm that it "breathes the air of eternity." The heavens declare his glory, the creation cries aloud that it has a divine source, a Maker, a Designer. Generation after generation rises and passes away, coming from the dust and returning to the dust. And "from everlasting to everlasting Thou art God!"

So that's a good place to begin. But we can't stop there, because we are earth-bound creatures, and change and decay are certainly visible around us. So this psalmist moves on toward the real point of his song. He prays that our knowing we have but a short span of years on this earth may do something in us. Let this knowledge spur us to look beyond the immediate problems and preoccupations of today. We are not created simply to live, breathe and die. God has a larger purpose, a grander and nobler use for us. He has made us for himself!

"Teach us . . . teach us . . . teach us"—what? To number our days. To remember that we do not have an unlimited lease on this earthly life, that its opportunities run out, that the time for doing good is *now*, and we have no sure claim on tomorrow. If we are wise, we will remember who we are now, and we will seek God's blessing and favor on our daily lives. We will remember that life is short and eternity is long. We will remember that God's blessing is promised on those who turn from their selfish ways and make him Lord of their lives. We will remember Jesus Christ, who died that we might have life, and have it more abundantly. And we will begin to live as those who have gotten "a heart of wisdom." The fear of the Lord is the beginning of wisdom, and those who fear the Lord need fear nothing else. He is a stronghold and protector of all who take their refuge in him.

Cultivating A Cheerful Spirit   OCTOBER 7

Psalm 111 and Ephesians 5:15-20

". . . Making melody to the Lord with all your heart, always and for everything giving thanks. . . ." EPHESIANS 5:19B AND 20A.

What kind of song do you sing? There are blues songs, dirges and laments over lost loves, torch songs, ballads, and so on. Then there are patriotic songs that bring memories of our heritage and the heroic deeds of the past. Some of us grew up on these songs in school. And finally, there are what the Bible calls "psalms, hymns and spiritual songs." These are songs that lift the spirit to realities we may too easily overlook.

Some people are blessed with a naturally cheerful outlook. Without too much effort they seem to be able to smile even when things are hard. Others of us have to work at doing so. Our natural disposition tends rather to be negative, perhaps anxious and fearful. So Paul's advice is especially aimed at people like us. We know that any worthwhile achievement requires some effort. Such is no less true of this most essential feature of life. What kind of spirit do we cultivate, and what kind of atmosphere do we seek to build around us? If we send forth negative, self-centered thoughts, the same will come back to us. If we want a different atmosphere, Paul shows us the way.

As soon as we allow the Holy Spirit within to begin a song of love and praise and thanksgiving to God, something basic happens.

> Flee, dark clouds that lower,
>   For my joy-bestower
>   Jesus, enters in!
> Joy from tribulation

Hope from desolation,
They who love God win.
Be it blame or scorn or shame
Thou art with me in earth's sadness,
Jesus, all my gladness!

Johann Frenck, 1650

A Steady Heart   OCTOBER 8

Psalm 112 and Hebrews 13:1-8

*He is not afraid of evil tidings; his heart is firm, trusting in the
Lord. His heart is steady.*   PSALM 112:7, 8A

One characteristic of an unsteady heart is fear. And the Bible has much to say about fear. "Though a host should encamp against me, my heart shall not fear" (Psalm 27:3). And in today's New Testament reading, "We can confidently say, the Lord is my helper, I will not be afraid. What can man do to me?" (Hebrews 13:6). These are not only testimonies by people who have faced fear and found faith stronger than fear. They are written to encourage us to believe that the same thing can happen to us.

But before we can have faith stronger than fear, we need to see and acknowledge that we do have fear. If we want a steadfast heart that is not afraid of evil tidings, and live by hope rather than hopelessness, then we need to admit our fear to God. He does not demand that we be brave and strong in ourselves. If we try that, we will sooner or later meet some condition that is too much for us. A friend of mine who is struggling with cancer said to me recently, "I know that there is pain that I cannot handle without God's help. I know that there are situations that I cannot face by myself." And knowing that, he is facing a very serious condition with what the world would call "courage." He has a steady heart.

There is no shame in being frightened if we take that fear and place it in God's hand. A steady heart is just an ordinary one that has learned to trust its heavenly Father. Every experience of our life is aimed at developing that "trust relationship." I believe that God wants this relationship for us even more than we want it for ourselves, and is ready to help. So take your heart—whatever state it may be in—to God. Ask him to make it a steady one.

Underneath — Borne Up   OCTOBER 9

Psalm 68 and Luke 8:26-39

Blessed be the Lord who daily bears us up; God is our salvation. Our God is a God of salvation; and to God, the Lord, belongs escape from death.   PSALM 68:19, 20

"Who daily bears us up!" "Give us this day our daily bread."

Ours is not a "once for all" experience with God, but a daily, ongoing one. It is a relationship that must be maintained lest we lose it. Paul says, "I die daily." And again he says, "Work out your own salvation with fear and trembling; for God is at work in you, both to will and to work for his good pleasure" (Philippians 1:12b).

But what a thought is this from the psalmist! "Blessed be the Lord who daily bears us up." The picture here is of those who must be borne up lest they fall. "Blessed be the Lord." Our daily need brings us back to the throne of grace. His answer to our need should bring us to the altar of praise, to make "the sacrifice of thanksgiving." Are we doing this consistently? The fruit of it will show in our life, and the cost of neglecting it will also eventually show.

I am convinced that the reason some Christians have such a hard time with their negative feelings and spend so much energy "spinning their wheels" on old patterns of sin or memories of the past is their neglect at this very point. The practice of thanksgiving, of blessing the Lord "at all times," has a very wholesome and positive result in the soul. God is not interested in keeping us bound to the past, however dark. He is not interested in seeing his children wallow in jealousy, feeling that their desires have been denied, feeling that they were born in the wrong place in the family. He is bidding us get up, get out of the mire, and move on with him. And the key to fighting the old, destructive feelings and memories lies here. "Blessed be the Lord who daily bears us up." He is carrying us through the places we cannot walk through by ourselves. He has not despised us, but has loved us with an undying love. Today we are being carried through whatever trials the day may bring. "Underneath are the everlasting arms."

Praise Every Morning   OCTOBER 10

Genesis 9:8-17 and Mark 1:9-15

I will remember my covenant which is between me and you and every living creature of all flesh.   GENESIS 9:15

God remembers. He remembers his intention when he set this universe in motion. He remembers that we are dust, and that we are frail, needy creatures. He remembers that he loves us. He remembers that his Son Jesus stood in the Jordan and saw the heavens open, declaring to him and to others that he was the beloved Son. We who believe in Jesus have been baptized into that love. We have been incorporated into his kingdom of love, and he has set his seal upon us. He remembers.

But, alas, we forget! We are a forgetful people, and (to be very truthful) as we grow older, we tend to forget more easily. I find that I can remember things that happened decades ago better than I can recall some things that happened last week—or even yesterday!

Of course it is good that we can forget some things. If we had to carry all our memories, they would be burdens too great to bear. So God gives us the gift of forgetting. Paul says, "Forgetting what lies behind . . . I press on toward the goal."

But remembering is important, for in remembering we are strengthened for today's needs. Remembering the ways in which God has blessed us strengthens our hearts to face whatever the day brings forth. Remembering and praising should be linked together. If we remember only to regret what we did, or feel bad about something that happened, remembering can feed grief or bitterness. But we can choose to remember and to praise.

I think we should be sure to praise God when the sky is cloudy as well as when the sun is shining bright. It is a way of saying to him that we are grateful for all the bright days and all the bright promises that he remembers and fulfills.

Hope Makes Bold   OCTOBER 11

II Corinthians 3:12-4:2 and Luke 7:28-36

Since we have such a hope, we are very bold.
II CORINTHIANS 3:12

What is this hope Paul is speaking about that makes him so bold? It is the hope that has come into his life through his faith in Jesus Christ. Something new was happening in the world. God was calling a people to himself by spreading the good news that Jesus had died, had risen again, and would return. If that was true, it was the most important word anyone had every heard! And it still is. Why? Because it has to do with ultimate reality, with life and death for every one of us.

Many of us have spent a good part of our life trying to "be good," to "be successful," or to have people love and respect us. We may have succeeded, or we may have been disappointed in the results of our effort. But here is something different. "We are being changed into his likeness from one degree of glory to another." What does that mean? It means that we are in a process. God is at work in us, right now, wherever we are, and whatever our circumstance. He has taken us just as we are, has loved us, has called us to himself, and now is in the process of changing us into the people we were created to be. We don't know exactly what that is, but we do know that Jesus Christ is our example. We see in him what human life can be, and by God's grace, will be when we are matured and complete.

Our hope points us to the future. Today is not the end. We are not yet "a finished product." But, we are "on the way." Our hope is in who Jesus Christ is, what he is to us, and what he promises for the future. "I know the thoughts I have toward you," says God, "thoughts of good and not of evil, to bring you to a desired end." The hymn writer says it this way,

> "In hope that sends a shining ray
> Far down the future's broadening way.
> In peace that only thou canst give,
> With thee, O Master, let me live."

Learning to Rejoice   OCTOBER 12

Isaiah 60:1-6 and Ephesians 3:1-12

*Then you shall see and be radiant, your heart
shall thrill and rejoice.* ISAIAH 60:5A

The prophet here is speaking to a people in exile. They have many things about which they could (and probably did) complain. Their lot was not always an easy or happy one. So the prophet turns his words to their need for encouragement. That, it seems to me, is always God's way. When things look dark or uncertain, listen for a reassuring, encouraging inner word from God. It is in these times of darkness that we are called to choose rejoicing rather than repining. Here is where our faith can make the difference between hope and despair. We are not victims, however difficult our circumstance may be at this moment. We are beloved, redeemed children of God, greatly and mercifully cared for by our heavenly Father. He never imposes more trials on us, nor allows a heavier burden, than is good for us.

Praying is hardly praying at all if our words are accompanied with fears and foreboding about the future. Our fears are an accusation against God's goodness and faithfulness, and they send forth negative messages even when we are saying nice things. So the prophet describes sons and daughters "coming from far," and to the Jewish parent, the future of the family was a primary concern. I believe that we can safely take our hopes and longings to God, who cares and who listens to our prayers.

Can we let the memory of God's faithfulness in the past give us an expectant attitude toward the future? I believe we can, if we choose to do it.

Passing Through the Wilderness OCTOBER 13

Deuteronomy 26:1-11 and Luke 4:1-13

*And Jesus . . . was led by the Spirit for forty days
in the wilderness.* LUKE 4:1-2

A few years ago, I had to spend the better part of a day driving through the desert. I will never forget the paradoxical sense of both beauty and barrenness I felt along that journey. Within the comfort of an air-conditioned automobile, I found it easy to be attracted by the boundless, rugged spaces. But one step out of the car revealed the deception of it all. It was unbearably hot and dry, and the desert itself offered little hope of refreshment. I was glad that I was only passing through.

Our reading from Luke's Gospel tells us of Jesus' experience in the wilderness prior to the start of his public ministry. He entered the desert for 40 days, not by mistake, but as an essential part of God's purpose for his life. There, he underwent all of the trials and temptations so common to every human being, yet without succumbing in even the slightest way. The writer to the Hebrews tells us that Jesus was made like us in every respect (except sin), and that because he has suffered and been tempted, he is able to help all who are tempted. (Hebrews 2:17-18; 4:14-16)

Jesus knows what our wildernesses are like. There is not a single experience of pain, sorrow, fear, loneliness, hardship or grief with which our Lord is not familiar and fully sympathetic.

But these words of the Gospel, and those from the Old Testament, hold for us an additional word of encouragement. Isn't it good to know that the wilderness was never the goal, only a stop along the way.

There comes a time when we must pass beyond the sorrows, the griefs and the hurts of our lives. We must let them go, so that we can get on with the journey ahead. And we must do this in the full and certain knowledge that the day will come when we will have passed through all the wildernesses of life. Then by "a mighty hand and an outstretched arm," God will bring us into "a land flowing with milk and honey." Until then, let's keep our spiritual feet moving.

The Sheltering God   OCTOBER 14

Genesis 15:1-12, 17-18 and Luke 13:31-35

How often would I have gathered your children together as a hen gathers her brood under her wings, and you would not! LUKE 13:34B

Sometimes we get so caught up in the problems and frustrations of life that we forget that we have a sheltering God who watches over us as tenderly and carefully as a mother hen caring for her brood. That was the image our Lord used as he wept over Jerusalem. His own people had refused to hear his loving words that warned of the destruction they were bringing on themselves and invited them to a life of blessedness. "How often would I have gathered you."

Life cannot always be what we would like it to be. Life includes storms as well as quiet times, the "dark night" as well as the sunny day. These are part of God's plan to shape and mold us for our eternal enjoyment of the life he has prepared for us.

Jerusalem sadly refused to be under Jesus' sheltering care. The question this story raises for us all is this: How am I refusing the sheltering of God? In what ways am I denying him the privilege of covering me with his loving care? If we stay angry at situations we cannot change, are we not saying to God, "No! I don't want your sheltering arms around me. I choose to stay miserable, no matter what you or others may try to do to change me!" And if we make that choice, God waits for us to change our minds. He will not force us against our wills.

Holman Hunt painted a very famous picture entitled "The Light of the World." The artist meant this picture to portray our hearts, and the way we respond to God's loving call. "How often would I have gathered you . . . and you would not." It is easy to grow callous when the Lord may be patiently waiting for us to let him in anew. Let us ask him to show us how we are shutting him out, or how we are refusing his loving, sheltering care.

No Turning Back   OCTOBER 15

I Kings 19:15-21, Galatians 5:1, 13-25 and Luke 9:51-62

Another said, "I will follow you, Lord; but let me first. . . ."
Jesus said to him, "No one who puts his hand to the plow and
looks back is fit for the kingdom of God."   LUKE 9:61A, 62

Jesus is dealing with our excuses. He confronts each one of us as the Lord, the true and only savior of mankind, and says to us: "Put all your trust in me, believe in me, in your hearts cling to me, and follow me. I am gentle and lowly and you will find inward rest. My yoke is easy and my burden is light."

But our nature does not accept that invitation very willingly. We may sing, "I'll go where you want me to go, dear Lord," but when the road leads where we do not want to go, we have a hard time meaning these words.

Jesus knew that. He warned his followers that to follow him meant taking up their own cross. What these words would mean practically was the crossing out of the old self-interests, self-will and self-love. And all of us, without exception, have an abundance of Self to be crossed out. And Self is very tricky. It disguises itself as good intentions, harmlessness, and innocence. But underneath its disguises, it is concerned with only one thing: itself, its comfort, its happiness, its plans, its well being.

Jesus says we need new hearts, new attitudes, new concerns. We need to become tender-hearted and merciful towards others, more concerned with their pain and need than our own. "I will follow you, Lord, but first. . . ." Delays. Excuses. Put offs. And Jesus simply says, "If you're serious about loving me, put self aside and seek God's will first." Everything else necessary will be added to you. God is not mean and stingy. He doesn't plan to rob you of everything that makes life meaningful. But those things must come second. Only God must be first. So don't turn back to the past, not even to other people for life's meaning, to memories that cannot really sustain you. Only God can do that.

Losing and Gaining   OCTOBER 16

I Kings 19:9-18 and Luke 9:18-24

Whoever would save his life will lose it; and whoever loses his life for my sake, he will save it.   LUKE 9:24

That verse has always bothered me. That is probably because I have been so bent on "saving" my life. At any rate, it is a troubling word, because it cuts across our natural inclinations and desires. Think of how much energy and thought we give to "preserving" our life when it seems threatened in any way. I speak not only of our physical life, but of our "way of life," which means having things the ways we want them, if at all possible!

In spite of this, we admire the heroes who "sit loose" to life and risk it for the sake of others. A recently-declared saint of the Roman Catholic Church was Father Maximilian Kolbe, a Polish priest who had been interned in a concentration camp during World War II. When it was decided to execute several of the prisoners because of some infraction of the "rules," an arbitrary choice was made. The list included a man with a family of small children, who asked for mercy for his family. At that point, Father Kolbe volunteered to take the man's place, and was allowed to do so.

I think it is a profound truth about life, that seeking to save our life is innately self-defeating. Sooner or later we find

that it doesn't work. "He who saves his life shall lose it."
That's just a fact, a reality about the way things are. But
there is another way open to us: "If you will turn over your
life to me," Jesus seems to be saying, "you will find the very
thing you have given away is restored in a different and more
wonderful way." There is inner satisfaction, there is a secret
joy, there is strength to go through whatever you have to.

What he said to his disciples holds true for us. Being willing to relinquish control of our lives is ultimately fulfilling.
His word is true and he will not fail!

Doing It God's Way OCTOBER 17

II Kings 5:1-14 and Mark 1:40-45

*So he went down and dipped himself seven times in the Jordan
according to the saying of the man of God.* II KINGS 5:14

Naaman, a valiant soldier of the king of Aram, had con-
tracted the most dreaded disease of that ancient time—
leprosy. This would, when it became known to others,
require his banishment from normal society. A little slave girl,
who had been captured in some earlier battle with Israel,
heard Naaman and his wife talking about this dreadful ailment. Although she was a captive, she had come to love her
master and mistress, and wanted to help. Remembering the
fame of the prophet Elisha, back in her home country, she
said, "Would that my lord were with the prophet that is in
Samaria! For he would recover him of his leprosy."

Naaman was informed, and following the normal way of
doing things, he told this to the king of Aram. So (as kings
are wont to do) he sent gifts to the king of Israel with the
implied demand that someone heal Naaman. The king of

Israel was thunderstruck. Cure someone of leprosy? The thought was preposterous. What was the king of Syria trying to do, find an excuse for another war? He rent his clothes in despair.

Elisha the man of God heard of all this, and sent word to the king with a sharp reminder that, in spite of all of Israel's unfaithfulness in worshipping other gods, God still had a prophet among his people! The king got word back to Naaman, who then came with many gifts to the door of the prophet's house. But instead, Elisha sent his servant out to the chariot with a single message: "Go and wash in the Jordan seven times, and you will be cleansed of the leprosy." Naaman was furious. What an insult! If washing in rivers was the way of cleansing, there were better rivers than the Jordan back home in Syria. But his servants reasoned with him, reminding him that if the prophet had asked him to do some great deed, he would have done it very willingly. "How much more, then," they said, "when he tells you, 'wash and be cleansed?'

Do you see yourself in Naaman? Do we not all see ourselves in wanting to protect our pride, even when are reduced to a state of utter need? We want all the good things God has for us, but we want them on our own terms. And God often says, "Do it my way." That way may involve humiliation, embarrassment, loss of dignity and pride. But if God is using these means to help us, then we are foolish, are we not, to hold on to our old opinions and our pride? Naaman reconsidered his haughty response to Elisha's word from the Lord and went down and washed seven times in the Jordan. And to his great joy, he was healed!

Who are the Blessed? OCTOBER 18

I Corinthians 1:18-31 and Matthew 5:1-12

Blessed are the poor in spirit, for theirs is the
kingdom of heaven. MATTHEW 5:3

Recently I heard of a woman who spent a week or so in the home of a young Christian couple as part of her own spiritual need. Although she had almost anything her heart could desire, she was still looking for something more. The couple with whom she was assigned to live for a few days were struggling financially. She said to a friend, "Their towels are frayed and they don't match. But they're *happy*!" To her it didn't make sense that one could be happy without having matching towels.

Recently I met a man who may not be alive by the time you read this. His body is riddled with cancer, and he is obviously in a lot of pain. His doctor did not expect him to live through the past summer. But the testimony he gave of how God was meeting him at every turn brought tears to the eyes of his hearers and hope to the hearts of many who might be fighting various fears.

These two incidences remind me of what our two Scriptures are saying today. Paul says that God has chosen the "nothings" of the world to share his glory. And Jesus says in his famous "Beatitudes" that it is the poor in spirit who are truly blessed. It is so easy to be beguiled by the spirit of the world into thinking that circumstances and possessions are the key to happiness. Many of the things we see and hear invite us to believe that having more is the answer to feeling better. This is not true. The answer to inner happiness and peace is letting go. But when we decide that we don't have to have these things, that having the hope, faith, and love that God gives us is better than having our own way, we can be truly blessed.

Costs and Crosses   OCTOBER 19

Psalm 1 and Luke 14:25-33

Whoever does not bear his own cross and come after me, cannot be my disciple. For which of you, desiring to build a tower, does not first sit down and count the cost, whether he has enough to complete it? LUKE 14:27, 28

Jesus never minced words. When someone wanted to be his follower, he did not hesitate to tell him that there would be a cost. He knew what others did not yet know, that there was a cross awaiting him, and that his followers had to be prepared for their own crosses, too.

A cross is an instrument of death. Our "crosses" are means of putting to death that which is in opposition to God. They are aimed at our self-will, the idea that we have a right to run our lives the way we want them.

Crosses interfere with the pleasantness of life. They come unplanned and unbidden, like a storm at midday. They interrupt life: a sudden illness; the loss of someone we love; the loss of a job; some plan that we had been making having to be cancelled. They take lots of forms, but they have one thing in common: they "cross us out."

Jesus says here that if we are to be his disciples we must be prepared to "bear our own cross." That means that we must learn to say Yes to whatever God allows to come into our lives. He only sends us those that are necessary to complete his work of love in our souls. We can believe that because it is true, and believing it makes it easier to say Yes.

Jesus Only   OCTOBER 20

Genesis 17:1-10 and MARK 9:1-9

And suddenly looking around they no longer saw anyone with them, but Jesus only.   MARK 9:8

Today's Gospel tells us the story of the Transfiguration. It stands in the Gospel as a kind of preview of Jesus' resurrection. Only three of the disciples were allowed to witness it—Peter, James and John. As usual, Peter was the spokesman for the group, and when they saw Jesus strangely and wonderfully "transfigured" before their eyes, with his garments so white that no bleach on earth could have whitened them, they were awestruck. As they watched, he was talking with Moses and Elijah about what was shortly to befall him in his suffering and death that lay ahead. Peter blurted out, "Master, it is well that we are here! Let us build three booths, one for you, one for Moses, and one for Elijah." The Gospel goes on to add, "He did not know what to say, for they were exceedingly afraid!" No answer from Jesus, but from the cloud of glory that surrounded them, a voice came, saying, "This is my beloved Son; listen to him." And then they noticed that there was no one with them "but Jesus only."

How easy it is to look at all kinds of distractions and get our eyes off the central figure. Peter, James and John needed to know that it was Jesus—not Moses and Elijah—who was to be the center and focus of their lives. How do we, in a practical way, obey this word, to see Jesus only and to listen to him? A friend of mine several years ago said that she had come to the point of seeing her life as coming directly from God in every circumstance. She put it like this: *No secondary causes.*

If we would see Jesus only, we could say, "Father, what are you saying to me by allowing this—or that—thing to happen to me? I don't understand you, but I do trust you!" The disciples had to go down from the Mount of Transfiguration, into the valley of need, of conflict, of uncertainty. They did not learn the lesson at once, but eventually they came to know that they could go through anything—as long as they kept their eyes on Jesus. And so can we.

One Thing Needful   OCTOBER 21

Colossians 1:21-29 and Luke 10:38-42

But the Lord answered her, "Martha, Martha, you are anxious and troubled about many things; one thing is needful. Mary has chosen the good portion, which shall not be taken away from her." LUKE 10:41, 42

I have always liked Martha in this Gospel story—probably because she is so much like us. Martha was concerned about practical things, like getting dinner on the table! Very few of us are like Mary by nature—choosing the better part easily and almost automatically.

I know people who not only fret about many things, but have actually raised such fretting to a level of virtue. They insist that if they did not worry about the details of this or that, things would not get done and everything would go to pot. Are you like that? Look about you, or think about your day. Do you have a kind of "worry quotient"—a certain amount of worrying you feel obliged to get done one way or another?

Jesus told Martha that Mary had chosen the "one thing needful." Somehow in her heart she had been able to distinguish between things that didn't matter at all and things that were important. There is a wonderful prayer which many people have found helpful. It goes like this: "Lord, help me to change the things that can be changed and to accept the things that cannot be changed, and the wisdom to know the difference."

Are we sorting out the needful from the trivial? Do we let little things loom too large in our lives? God's peace is all around us, and certainly can be within us, for Jesus has said, "My peace I give to you." But we will miss that peace if we choose to fret and fume over every little thing. We have choices, as Mary and Martha did. Somehow, I think Martha learned to make the better choice. And I am trying to learn that important lesson day by day!

Eternal Comfort and Good Hope   OCTOBER 22

II Thessalonians 2:13-3:5 and Luke 20:27-38

Now may our Lord Jesus Christ himself, and God our Father,
who loved us and gave us eternal comfort and good hope
through grace, comfort your hearts and establish them in every
good work and word.   II THESSALONIANS 2:16, 17

We cannot live a truly human life without hope. When hope is gone, we turn into self-absorbed creatures. For hope focuses our attention beyond the needs of the moment and enables us to live beyond ourselves.

A friend of mine died recently after a long battle with cancer. During the years of the illness, there were many very painful treatments. Hopes for recovery rose, only to be dashed by an aggressive return of the disease. But through it all a strange and wonderful thing happened. Hope, real hope, grew in his heart. There was something worth living for, because God had given him hope for the life that is to be. Suffering would end, his body would one day cease to live, but he, the person, would go on living with God. That was hope, and it was alive right up to his death. Paul is saying that God has given us "eternal comfort and good hope." If our eyes are not fixed on eternity and the reality of the life beyond, the immediate can become very demanding, even tyrannical. So in the loving kindness of God, he has given us that hope and comfort. It is ours through our faith and trust in Jesus Christ, and by the indwelling Spirit of God in our hearts. "Eternal comfort and good hope." What a gift!

Weary in Well-Doing?   OCTOBER 23

II Thessalonians 3:6-13 and Luke 21:5-19

Brethren, do not be weary in well-doing. II THESSALONIANS 3:13

That was Paul's advice to the Christians of his day. He knew that for some of them the battle of life was difficult, and they were tempted to give up their struggle. Weariness is a matter of fatigue, and we all know how that feels.

Paul is not talking about physical weariness, however. It was "soul weariness" he was concerned about—a flagging of zeal, a letting up of the desire to stay near God. One of the areas in which we can grow "soul-weary" is in our compassion for others. Remembering how difficult we can be for others can make us more merciful to those who annoy us. "Do not be weary in well-doing."

Another area in which we grow weary is in facing our own faults. It is one thing to recognize that we have faults we don't like. It is quite another thing to try to overcome them. Human nature is so stubborn, our patterns are so ingrained, that we find ourselves slipping back into old reactions we thought we had overcome long ago. And that can be very discouraging.

The most refreshing thing I know is to remember that we are greatly loved, often forgiven, and that the Holy Spirit makes possible for us what we could never achieve for ourselves. We are not left to struggle by ourselves. He is with us and in us. "Do not grow weary."

Putting Off and Putting On   OCTOBER 24

Exodus 16:2-4, 12-15 and Ephesians 4:17-24

Put off your old nature. . . . And put on the new nature. . . .
EPHESIANS 4:22, 24

The Christian life is a putting off and a putting on. It is a life of continual and constant change. And that's what makes it so exciting and so difficult.

Jesus told about needing new wineskins for new wine, for he said that new wine would burst the old skins, and everything would be lost. He was talking about the effect of the new life he came to bring us. It would burst open the old ways, and if people didn't get "new skins" (which means if they were not willing to change their ways), everything would be lost.

Jesus also reminded us that when the new comes, it is more comfortable to keep with the old. After all, even if the old way is not so good, somehow we've learned to live with it. Then comes the disturbing moment when something inside says, "Wake up! Time is short and you need to change. Things are not the way God wants them."

Too many of us stop "half-way" and don't let the changing process continue, because we are more comfortable with the "way we've always been." Don't despair! We can change because God has given us the grace and power to do so though Jesus Christ.

First, however, you must find out if you think you need to change. Then talk to God about it. Tell him what you don't like about yourself, and ask him to begin the change in you. Be very honest and don't hold back, and keep doing that every day. Second, ask forgiveness for anything wrong that comes to your mind. Third, expect that you are going to become a new person. That is faith. It is believing that Jesus Christ can do what he said, and that he will do it.

I Press On   OCTOBER 25

I Kings 19:1-8, Philippians 3:7-14 and Matthew 17:1-9

Not that I have already obtained this or am already perfect,
but I press on to make it my own, because Christ Jesus has
made me his own. PHILIPPIANS 3:12

There is a lot to be said for "pressing on." A race is not won by a quick start, but by the perseverance that holds out to the end. And life has its need for such perseverance.

How easy it is to become discouraged along the way! We suffer disappointments, setbacks of all kinds, griefs, hurts—and most of all, we fail to live up to the things we most desire and believe in.

Elijah felt that way after his encounter with the priests of Baal on Mount Carmel, proving to all that the Lord is God and that Baal is not God. But Elijah was tired. Standing alone is not easy! Then Queen Jezebel sent him word that she would have him done in by the next day. That was too much, and Elijah ran for his life. When he got down to the broom tree in the wilderness, he prayed, "Lord, take away my life. It is enough!" We can understand Elijah's feeling of wanting to give up.

We cannot afford to give in to such feelings. They will rob us of that which God desires to give us, and they will keep us from the fulfillment he desires to bring into our lives. Such feelings, if we indulge them, will rob others of the blessing we can be to them as well. So we must press on.

What does that mean? For Paul, it meant that he was aware of his shortcomings, his failures, and his unconquered areas. God was still at work in him and with him, and Paul knew that it was all worthwhile. For you and me this should be a word of great encouragement. By God's grace, we too can press on!

He Will Speak Peace   OCTOBER 26

Psalm 85:8-13 and Isaiah 40:1-11

*Let me hear what God the Lord will speak, for he will speak
peace to his people. . . .*   PSALM 85:8A

When God speaks to us, his word brings peace. That is the encouraging word I would share with all of you who read this. When God speaks to us, his word brings peace. There is a prayer that I love which reads like this:

> Be present, O Merciful God, and protect us
> through the silent hours of this night; so
> that we who are wearied by the changes and

chances of this world may rest on Thy eternal
changelessness; through Jesus Christ our Lord.

I commend it to you, even to memorize if you feel so
inclined. Surely amid the wearisome changes and chances of
this world we all need that sure anchor of God's changelessness. Let's think for a few moments about what that peace is
which he speaks to us. First, there is a sense of rest and ease
with God and with ourselves. Sometimes his word is a sharp
word, piercing our hearts with stabbing awareness of how
wrong we have been—how neglectful, how stubborn, how
opinionated, how self-righteous, how unloving. And when
he gets through into our inmost being with the sharp edge of
truth, it may be painful. But then there comes the joyful
awareness that we are forgiving, that we do not have to live
with guilt and vain regret—and with that comes a new sense
of "at-one-ness" with God and ourselves.

Second, this peace which God speaks makes us content
with circumstances we cannot change. Suffering is an
inevitable part of our life here, and we waste it if we simply
fight against it. Suffering may consist in being where we
would not choose to be, or having conditions in our lives
which are very contrary to our desires. Yet if our circumstances cannot be changed, we need to come to peace by sub-
mitting to a will higher than our own. God will speak to our
inward heart if we listen very carefully to his still, small
voice.

How does God's word to us bring peace? By stilling the
storm of contrary winds within and enabling us to link our
will to his. He is the Master, and with his help we can face
all the outward tumults, if his calm is within.

The Question and the Answer OCTOBER 27

Romans 7:14-25A and Matthew 11:25-30

Wretched man that I am! Who will deliver me from
this body of death? ROMANS 7:24

Come unto me, all who labor and are heavy-laden.
MATTHEW 11:28A

Thank God for Paul's honesty! In this remarkable seventh chapter of Romans he describes a condition which every one of us could identify with: we don't understand ourselves! "I do not do the good I want, but the evil I do not want is what I do."

Paul was aware of this "split" inside himself, and it had brought him to despair. At one time he had thought that being "good" was enough to satisfy God and assure him of a place in heaven. Then, by confrontation with Jesus on the road to Damascus, he saw that his "goodness" wasn't really goodness at all in God's sight. We all need to see that. Our good behavior is not what God is looking for. He is looking at our heart. If we have come, like Paul, to confess that we don't even live up to our own standards, then we're ready to hear what Jesus has to say to us.

"Come to me, all who labor and are heavy-laden." There is the answer to that old problem. He wants us to return to him. He wants us to bring those feelings and problems, those confusions and conflicts, those fears and worries to him. He does not wait to judge or condemn us, but to give us rest. That's what he said, and that's what he meant.

God at Work In You   OCTOBER 28

Philippians 2:9-13 and Luke 2:15-21

Work out your own salvation with fear and trembling, for God is at work in you, both to will and to work for his good pleasure.
PHILIPPIANS 2:12B, 13A

It is good to recall the truth of this text: God is at work in us. Left to ourselves, we could be frightened about the prospects ahead of us. The future is unknown, and for many who read these lines, it undoubtedly holds some concern.

In writing these words to the Philippian Christians, Paul is anxious that they not lose perspective on where things are with them. Although they have to face daily temptations and circumstances beyond their control, they need to be reminded that God is still in charge of their lives and that he is still at work in them. What an encouraging thought that is!

God is at work in you both to will and to work for his good pleasure. Since we are so bound by our human nature to think first of ourselves and our own interests, God has graciously entered our lives, working in us "to will" that which is pleasing to him.

Then as we allow his work to continue in us, we are being changed. The old passes away and the new comes. We are counselled to "Put on the Lord Jesus Christ and make no provision for the flesh" (Romans 13:14). That means that as we cooperate with him, an inward change is taking place.

I find that as I grow older, I am having to face fears that I was able to ignore in my earlier life. The fear was always there, but when things were going well, and I was physically well and strong, the fear was not so apparent. But when there are evidences that the body is less able to cope with the things that happen to it, fear becomes a real enemy. It is good to remember when fear pops up that "God is at work."

He hasn't left the scene. He is still there with us and in us. Call out to him when you feel afraid. The future is in his hands. His love will never diminish, no matter what. And he will not give up on us. What a savior!

Do Whatever He Tells You OCTOBER 29

Isaiah 62:1-5 and John 2:1-11

[Jesus'] mother said to the servants, "Do whatever he tells you."
JOHN 2:5

This wonderful story of Jesus' first miracle in Cana of Galilee gives us a rare glimpse of his relationship with his mother. She was obviously connected with his ministry at various stages, because the Gospel writers mention her from time to time, along with the other women "that ministered to him."

Here we can see an eager (even anxious) mother, who wanted her Son to live up to his calling. She knew that he was a special child, and that God had given him to her to bring up "in the nurture and admonition of the Lord." She also must have known something of his power, for she went to him when the marriage feast was floundering for lack of wine. In that culture a celebration of that kind included so many people (even strangers) that it would be considered a great failure of hospitality to run out of wine at this critical point.

Thus, in complete confidence that the matter would be taken care of, Mary said to the servants, "Do whatever he tells you." There can be no better advice given to any of us, no matter what our situation may be. It may be as impossible as that Cana situation, because, humanly speaking, things were at a standstill.

Many, many times our lives come to such a standstill. We cannot see how things will "work out." We have come, as the old verse says, "to wit's end's corner." And that is when we need to go to him, as Mary did, with our need, with our impossibilities, with our fear, with our anxiety. And then we need to listen. Listen within, to what he says in our hearts. Always he bids us believe, trust, hope and lift up our hearts. You can't go wrong with that!

Not Far from the Kingdom   OCTOBER 30

Deuteronomy 6:1-9 and Mark 12:28-34

And when Jesus saw that he answered wisely, he said to him,
"You are not far from the kingdom of God."   MARK 12:34A

We do not know what became of the man to whom Jesus spoke these words. The record does not tell us. He was a scribe, one of a professional class of "exponents and teachers of the law." It was his calling to teach others the way of life.

This particular scribe asked a question that must have been asked many times: Which is the greatest commandment? In his reply, Jesus in effect underscored the question. Then come the words of our text: When Jesus saw that he answered wisely, he said to him, "You are not far from the kingdom of God." Think about those words, and what they might mean to us.

First, he came to the right place to ask his question. This man went to the Lord. Second, he asked the right question. We should not waste time asking frivolous questions—about God, about the Bible, about ourselves, even about our future. Ask the right question: Lord, what is important for me today? Finally, he listened when he got an answer. When we go to the Lord in prayer concerning some question or problem, do we listen, really listen inwardly to hear what he might say to us? I think we would all be very wise to do more inward listening, for prayer must be a two-way street.

Jesus rightly saw that this scribe's attitude brought him very near the kingdom. The kingdom of God is the rule of God in our lives, when we turn over to him the reins of our heart. Like Mary, we say to him, "Let it be to me according to your word."

Thy Servant Heareth   OCTOBER 31

Samuel 3:1-10 and John 1:35-42

And the Lord came and stood forth, calling as at other times, "Samuel, Samuel." And Samuel answered, "Speak, for thy servant hears." I SAMUEL 3:10

The lad Samuel did not recognize God's voice when he first spoke to him. He needed the help of the aged Eli to know that it was indeed God who was speaking. The main point for us is that Samuel was ready to hear what the Lord was saying to him. And when he was ready, he understood what God wanted him to hear. I think most of us do not take seriously the fact that God still speaks, still communicates his will to us. For usually God speaks in a "still, small voice," not in thundering tones to be heard by everyone around us.

God speaks through inspired thoughts that come into our minds. St. Paul says that no one can say "Jesus is Lord" [and mean it] "except by the Spirit." What he is saying is that the Holy Spirit gives rise to the conviction that Jesus is indeed Lord, and so enables us to say with our lips that great saving confession. "If you confess with your mouth the Lord Jesus, and believe in your heart that God raised him from the dead, you shall be saved" (Romans 10:9). Thanks be to God who inwardly speaks to us and gives us the faith to make that goodly confession!

Again, God may put in our minds the thought of doing a loving act for someone, or bring some wrong act or some attitude to our minds so that we can confess it. Or again he may remind us that we need to forgive someone for some wrong or hurt he or she has done to us. God also speaks to us through other people. Samuel had a message for Eli about God's judgment upon his family. John the Baptist called people to change their ways of thinking and living to get ready for the kingdom or rule of God. There have always been those who were called especially to be God's prophets, or spokesmen, to bear a message to his people.

But sometimes he speaks to us through a friend, a relative, a doctor or nurse. Anyone who tells us the truth is, in a sense, "speaking for God." We can receive it as from God, no matter who says it to us. What we need is a ready, listening ear. "Speak, for your servant hears."

God also speaks to us through his holy Word, the Bible. As we read its inspired words, there is life, health, quickening, forgiveness and hope in them. God who inspired them guards them, and the Holy Spirit quickens them to us as we read them in faith. Quiet times can be listening times, when you turn your heart to hear God's word to you. He is always more ready to speak than we are to hear, so let us do our part, that we may be blessed by whatever he will say to our hearts. With the poet Miss Havergal, we can pray, "Lord, speak to me, that I may speak in living echoes of Thy tone." We will be blessed by whatever he has to say to us, and we can be a blessing to others if we become faithful listeners to his voice.

He Will Do It

For to us a child is born,
to us a son is given, and the
government will be on his
shoulders. And he will be called
Wonderful Counselor, Mighty
God, Everlasting Father, Prince
of Peace. Of the increase of his
government and peace there
will be no end. He will reign
on David's throne and over his
kingdom, establishing and
upholding it with justice and
righteousness from that time
on and forever. The zeal of
the Lord Almighty will
accomplish this.

ISAIAH 9:6-7 (NIV)

Wedding Moments

"May the Lord lift up his countenance upon you and give you his peace, this day and even forever more. *Amen.*" The words flowed effortlessly, a consequence of doing many weddings, but the lump in his throat and the film of moisture that blurred his vision betrayed the emotion that welled up inside. This one was different.

His son turned hesitantly to his new bride, squeezed her hand, kissed her carefully and embraced her gently. She responded in kind, sensing a certain specialness in the moment. She was comfortable and secure in the embrace, but there was also a sense of excitement that something in their relationship was new. They separated and turned. She hooked her arm in his, and with broad smiles for each other and those assembled, they made their way down the long aisle.

His heart was full as he watched them disappear into the vestibule. His son had never been happier in all his twenty-nine years. As the first child he had borne the consequences of generational insecurity and a father trying to do everything right. This pressure plus that of growing up under the scrutiny reserved for ministers' children had molded him into a serious, purposeful young man—one who had become an officer and a helicopter pilot in the United States Marine Corps. He was very proud of his son, but often felt a nebulous guilt wondering if it was his fault his son was so intense. He wished that he could relax and enjoy and accept himself more fully.

"The bride is a delight; full of life, enthusiasm and love. She laughs easily, is very bright and has energy to spare. She is good for him. She helps him laugh, and feel, and he is softer and more at peace since he met her." He was grateful for her strengths, and for her love for his son.

His thoughts were interrupted as his wife left the church. Escorted down the aisle by the best man, their younger son, she looked terrific in her elegant green dress. He was grateful for her. If his son's bride would be as good for his son as his wife of 31 years had been for him. . . . "Lord make it so. . . ."

The congregation, moving quickly now, followed the wedding party out of the church and on to the reception. So many weddings over the years. So many hopes and dreams . . . so many dangers and pitfalls. "Make this one different, Lord." He wished he could capture the moment, the sense of God's love in the love they had felt for each other when they had kissed at the altar. He wished he could hold them in that state forever, or at least remind them of it when the inevitable stresses of marriage came up. He wished he could protect them from all the difficult things they would face together. He knew that he couldn't. He prayed, "Lord bless them . . . really bless them." Then he turned, and with a full heart returned to the sacristy.

Bill Dubocq

He Gives His Beloved Sleep   NOVEMBER 1

Psalm 127 and Matthew 23:1-12

It is in vain that you rise up early and go late to rest, eating the bread of anxious toil; for he gives to his beloved sleep.
PSALM 127:2

You and I walk the path of life in a great company. It does not matter whether we see it or not, whether we can get out to be with the throngs that go to God's house on Sunday. These are our companions on the way, our friends in the Spirit, our fellow sisters and brothers in the family of God. There are the prophets, apostles, evangelists, martyrs, and pioneers of faith like Abraham. There are missionaries, the scholars who preserved the precious truths of God, and then there are the fathers and mothers who schooled their children in the faith, the young and the old—what a blessed company indeed we travel with in this pathway of faith!

Today is called "All Saints' Day" as a way of recalling to mind whose company it is we travel in. It is appropriate on this special holy day to remember the rest from our labors he has promised to those who love him. We can rejoice with them in the hope of a life that goes on—not just in length of days, but in happy fulfillment of all that is promised in God's creative and redemptive plan.

There is another meaning here that should not escape us. One of the original meanings of this text may have been "He gives to his beloved in sleep"—meaning while they sleep. Have you thought of how many times God speaks to us as we sleep? In our unguarded state, he gives us what we are incapable of receiving when we are awake and active. So we must be grateful for his gift of sleep and for what he gives us in sleep.

To Follow Him   NOVEMBER 2

Jonah 3:1-5, 10 and Mark 1:14-20

And immediately he called them; and they left their father
Zebedee in the boat with the hired servants, and followed him.
MARK 1:20

This short incident in the Gospel of Mark is important—
not only for the apostles, but for us. First, notice that
Jesus called them to come with him. They were going about
their business as usual, and they may have had no thought of
the decision they would soon be called to make. But Jesus did
come down and walk into their lives and call them, and after
that things were never the same. It should be so with us.

Whether the Lord came into our lives when we were very
young or when we were older, his coming and his call should
make all the difference. For when he calls us it is to a new
purpose and a new goal. No longer are we to be mere time-
servers, mere workmen, housewives, students—whatever—
seeking our own private plans and goals. We are called to
enlist in the King's host—the company which stretches all
the way back to Jesus and the Apostles—and even beyond—
to patriarchs, prophets, the faithful souls of all ages! If you
have never answered that call definitely and positively in
your heart, it is still not too late to do so. Just say, "Yes, Lord
Jesus."

The second thing that this text says to us is that the disciples had to leave something behind. In their case it was
their father, Zebedee, who was probably the owner of the
fishing operation. "Leaving their father Zebedee in the boat
with the hired men. . . ." That meant a step of great faith on
their part. They couldn't serve two masters, so in order to be
faithful to the call of Jesus, they had to leave their old ways

behind. For us it may be giving up old plans, old associations, old dreams, old ambitions—to seek a kingdom that will go on for ever. For all of us, it will undoubtedly mean forsaking something that we've held dear.

The third thing this text says is that the disciples went off to follow him. People follow many different leaders. They model their lives after all kinds of heroes. Jesus calls us to follow him. "Take my yoke upon you, and learn of me," he says. To follow him means to learn to live with the same goals he had, to seek the same desires that moved him, with the same obedience he showed in his life. It is a call to live with him day by day. Let's answer "Yes" to his call.

But Say the Word NOVEMBER 3

I Kings 8:22-23, 41-43, Galatians 1:1-10 and Luke 7:1-10

"Lord, do not trouble yourself, for I am not worthy to have you come under my roof. Therefore I did not presume to come to you. But say the word, and let my servant be healed." LUKE 7:6B, 7

The centurion was a Roman officer in charge of a hundred soldiers. His task and that of his men was to keep peace by keeping the subjected Jews from rising up. Undoubtedly he had been reared in one of the religions of the time—but no mention is made in the Gospel of his personal background. In the midst of his work in Galilee, he had come to have great respect for the faith of the Jews. And so, as an act of personal faith and generosity, he had built a synagogue in Capernaum where he was stationed. Visitors to the Holy Land tell us that much of that structure still stands, a kind of preserved witness to God's acceptance of his offering.

But the centurion is remarkable in two ways: he understood authority and he recognized a divine authority in Jesus. He knew what it was to obey his military superiors, and how to command those under him. That was a good foundation for his understanding of Jesus. The centurion sensed that Jesus carried Divine Power within him, and there was an authority about him over the winds and waves—and all human conditions—including the sickness of his beloved slave. And so he came—saying, "Don't trouble yourself to come to my house, Lord; I'm not worthy to have you step under my roof. But just say the word. . . ."

Jesus still has authority over conditions of all kinds. We can still take our needs to him in the confident faith that he will hear us and answer us according to what is best for us. Above all, he will come "under our roof," to abide in us and with us, to help us in the hard times, to cheer us when we are down, to help us see when we are wrong, and to lead us forward toward the fulfillment of God's great, loving purpose for us.

Like the centurion, let us summon all the faith resources we have, and say to Jesus, "Here, Lord, is my need. Just say the word. . . ."

The Light of His Glory   NOVEMBER 4

II Corinthians 4:3-6 and Mark 9:2-8

It is God . . . who has shone in our hearts to give the light of the knowledge of the glory of God in the face of Jesus Christ.
II CORINTHIANS 4:6

In today's Gospel, three of Jesus' disciples were allowed to get a preview of the resurrection. They saw Jesus "transfigured" before them, an awesome sight they never forgot.

All of a sudden, his glory shone through his earthly figure, and they knew that he was truly the Son of God.

Paul talks about a different but no less awesome sight: the light of his glory shining in our hearts. One cannot describe exactly what this means. Different people talk about it in different ways, and most of us don't really talk about it at all. But when there is that quickening glimpse of God's love, of his mercy, of his glory, we are "seeing" him in our hearts.

At times we all feel dull and lifeless inside. We do not have the warmth and burning desire for God that we know we should, and we are often preoccupied with the most trivial matters. During a recent illness, I was shocked at how preoccupied I would become with the most petty things. Too much laughter at the table, too much noise, the wrong TV program—things that should have meant nothing to me would seem *very* important. Even some innocent remark from my wife or a friend could set off a whole string of pointless thinking. When we are wrapped up in ourselves, the heart really does become dull and cold.

"The glory of God in the face of Jesus." I love a word I read not long ago that described faith as simply looking at Jesus. And the writer said that when we look at his face, it is always a loving face, caring for us. When we see that face, we see the glory of God in a way we can understand. It is not just a bright shining light, but it is a welcoming one. It is not just brilliant shining glory, but a warm assuring look that bids us believe that he will not fail us, no matter how rough the path may be at the moment. "It is God . . . who has shone . . . in the face of Jesus Christ."

Waiting for God   NOVEMBER 5

Psalm 62 and Mark 1:14-20

*For God alone my soul waits in silence; for
my hope is from him.*   PSALM 62:5

Waiting isn't as bad as I used to think it was. I have
always been a very impatient person. I can remember
even as a child, trying to wheedle my mother into showing
us our Christmas presents before Christmas!

But God has ways of dealing with us. For me, much of
the year 1996 was spent in waiting to recover from two serious operations just a month and a half apart. Waiting to
recover from another life-threatening illness that left me
weak and shaky, and made it hard to concentrate for very
long. Waiting to get better; waiting to get stronger.
Sometimes waiting impatiently, and sometimes, as the
psalmist says, "waiting in silence."

There come times in all our lives when the action slows
down or even ceases. We are called, perhaps, to step aside
and allow others to march on. We are called to "wait in
silence" to see how God is going to deal with our situation.
One thing we can be sure of: He is not going to leave us
alone. He is not going to abandon us just because we cannot
be carrying the load that once was ours to bear. "Even to
your old age I am he. And to gray hairs I will carry you"
(Isaiah 46:4).

It is easy to grow bitter when we have to go through
these waiting times. Here is a word we all need: "For God
my soul waits in silence, for my hope is from him." Unless
we allow these periods to renew and strengthen our hope,
we will inevitably become frightened and bitter. But we have
a choice! Because Jesus Christ is alive, because he loves us

and wants us to have a plentiful, abundant life even in the waiting times, we can choose to put our hope in him.

The Miracle of Forgiveness   NOVEMBER 6

Isaiah 43:18-25 and Mark 2:1-12

*I am he who blots out your transgressions for my own sake, and
I will not remember your sins.*   ISAIAH 43:25

. . . The Son of Man has authority on earth to forgive sins. . . .
MARK 2:10

Both Scripture readings this week have to do with the greatest miracle and the greatest gift we could possibly experience from God—the forgiveness of sins. Of course, we don't usually think of that as a miracle. But did you ever stop to think how hard it is to forgive a real wrong or hurt? Not just a little thing, but something that went to the very core of your being. Didn't you find it a real struggle to release the wrongdoer from the punishment you felt in your heart he or she richly deserved?

The Bible tells us that sin is an offense against God, and that "we have all sinned and fallen short of the glory of God." Further, it teaches us that sin is basically rebellion against the rule of God, and that from the first human beings until now, rebellion against God has been part of our human nature.

It is not that we set out consciously to become rebels; rather it is simply that we are rebellious, and because of this we have often disobeyed and displeased God. Jesus Christ is God's answer to our sin problem. He became human and tasted our human life to the full. Then he offered back to

God the obedience and love which humanity owed, and God accepted that offering in our behalf. In this wonderful way, Jesus has opened the way back to God for all of us, and offers us a way to a restored relationship with our heavenly Father. He offers us the forgiveness of our sins, because he has made a perfect sacrifice in our behalf.

When we face our true condition and accept his forgiveness, we have the wonderful assurance that we are restored to a new relationship with him. We are brought to "at-one-ment" (atonement)—into a loving, free relationship as his children. What higher gift could we imagine, and what greater miracle could there be?

We need never be afraid, ashamed or reluctant to confess our sins and ask forgiveness with a humble heart. The Father waits to bless a thousandfold any child of his who comes in such need.

To Whom Shall We Go?   NOVEMBER 7

Joshua 24:1-2A, 14-25 and John 6:60-69

. . . Choose this day whom you will serve.   JOSHUA 24:15B

*. . . Lord, to whom shall we go? You have the words
of eternal life.*   JOHN 6:68

Today's Scriptures are about choices. The people of Israel were entering into the Promised Land, facing the battles that still had to be fought, and they had to decide whether they were going to love and serve the Lord who had brought them from Egypt, or whether they would "buy into" the religions of the people around them. Joshua was concerned that they make a good choice, because their future welfare depended on it.

Jesus faced a time in his earthly ministry when some of his disciples were turning away. He was saying things they thought were too hard. At that point, he turned to the Twelve, and asked them, "Will you go away also?" There was no indication that he would change his message to make it more like what the world wanted to hear. But he did recognize that every disciple had a choice to make. Peter spoke for the group when he answered, "Lord, to whom shall we go? You have the words of eternal life."

I'm sure that you are aware, as I am, how easy it is to start putting your hopes and your faith in the wrong thing. Even good things can sometimes get in the way of really putting our whole heart's trust in Jesus Christ. So it's important to hear his words, to study and inwardly digest them, so that we place our trust wholly in him and not in ourselves.

It may be that you made your decision long ago to love God and to trust in Jesus Christ as your Lord and Savior. Or it may be that you need to make that conscious decision now, with your eyes fully open to the disappointing results of living for any other goal than serving him. In either case, the decision must be made in a practical, day-to-day way, in the context of where you are now. I believe he wants to be more to all of us than we have allowed him to be. I believe he wants to give us an inner fulfillment and joy we can't find anywhere else, even if we chase the whole world over. So in light of that, I read those words of Joshua: "Choose this day." And I read Peter's words, "Lord, to whom shall we go? You have the words of eternal life."

What Jesus Wants of Us   NOVEMBER 8

Deuteronomy 18:15-20 and Mark 1:21-28

And he cried out, "What have you to do with us, Jesus of Nazareth? Have you come to destroy us?" MARK 1:24A

This has always been a fascinating story—one of the first exorcisms the Gospels describe in the ministry of Jesus. An exorcism is the act of "driving out demons." In this particular incident the unclean spirit is described as speaking through the man. "What do you want with us?" The answer is a two-fold one.

First, Jesus had come to destroy the work and effect of evil within the man. He came to destroy the works of the devil, according to I John 3:8. That was the underlying motive of his incarnation—to set things right that had long been wrong in this poor world. In every glimpse we have of Jesus in the Gospels, he is busy about his Father's business—healing, casting out unclean, destructive spirits, giving sanity and wholeness and inner healing where there had been darkness, disease and despair. Jesus is the mighty Conqueror of Satan, and on the cross he would meet the foe in its fiercest form. But the power of the evil one could not defeat the Conqueror, and by his death, freely given for us, he has provided our deliverance.

The second answer to that man's question is a positive one. For Jesus had come not only to banish the evil spirit, but to bring freedom and life to the man. Every one of us can echo those words as we meet the Healing Christ—whatever our need. But when he begins to work in us, we may feel as this man did—that he is going to take too much away from us! How many people have turned away from Jesus because they thought they would have to give up too much if they really became his followers? What we all need to remember is that he said, "I came that they might have life and have it more abundantly!" He does not come to destroy anything that is good. He comes to take away that which does destroy, so that the abundant life may be ours. So do not fear or draw back—whatever God may be doing in your life at this moment. Do not think that he has come to make your life empty, meaningless or unhappy. It is his intention to fill you with a life that is new every day. Most of us only come to realize this fact a little at a time, but that is what the Lord is seeking to do in our lives—right now.

The Set of the Mind   NOVEMBER 9

Ezekiel 37:1-14 and Romans 8:6-11

To set the mind on the flesh is death, but to set the mind on the Spirit is life and peace.   ROMANS 8:6

First of all, let us make sure we understand what the Apostle Paul means by the word "flesh." As Paul is using it here, the word sums up that entire aspect of our life which is ungodly, separated from God and his will. Perhaps you know people, as I do, who constantly have little complaints about their lot.

Ezekiel saw that vision of a valley filled with dry bones. No life. Everything that would give life was missing. And then, in obedience to the Lord, he prophesied, and life came. The point is that when God's Spirit came upon the dry, dead human condition, life sprang into being.

And when we allow God to come into our deadness and dryness, a true miracle happens. Without any outward change, everything changes!

That's a wonderful thought for us whenever we seem dry and dead, lifeless and hopeless, somewhat down-in-the-mouth. We know the Source from which new life can come. If we pray, seek, know, and wait—the Spirit will move in our hearts, and old bitternesses, old fears, old lonelinesses will pass away and something wonderful will happen. The Lord has promised it will be so.

Paul said, "To set the mind on the Spirit is life and peace." So if you have a lot of deadness in your heart, ask him to give you a new mind-set. Set your mind on the Spirit. Seek and find that life and peace which he has promised. You can have it, for God says so!

Be Prepared   NOVEMBER 10

Amos 5:18-24 and Matthew 25:1-13

Watch therefore, for you know neither the day nor the hour.
MATTHEW 25:13

The point of Jesus' parable was that five of the brides-maids (the foolish virgins) lost their sense of priorities and allowed themselves to be distracted from their real purpose. Then when the "chips were down," so to speak, they weren't ready.

How like us! At least, I speak from personal experience. It's easy to let our surroundings draw us off track, so that we miss the very thing we're supposed to be doing. If this is true in small things, alas, it is even more true in the long haul of life. Do you know people who started out as young people to dedicate themselves to Jesus Christ, who made the goodly confession, began to live for him—only to become distracted by the cares and appeals of the world?

Unless we remember that we are here as children of God, that our main purpose is to love and serve and worship him forever, it will be very easy to be totally occupied with the frets and cares of life. It takes a conscious decision to turn away from these distractions to gaze upon eternity. It takes a conscious decision to be prepared inwardly for the hard times we all have to face.

The miracle of grace and the burden of this message is that, even now—though we may find ourselves woefully unprepared for what life is throwing at us—it is not too late to turn to him. He ever waits to bless, and longs to have us take up the weapons of our battle anew: faith, hope and love.

Why not make a new start today? Why not confess whatever failure, whatever lack of preparation you know is there—and ask him to begin to prepare you for whatever lies ahead. His strength and his grace are enough. But we have the privilege and responsibility of staying in touch with the Source of supply, so that when the testing time comes, we will be prepared.

Not As Man Sees NOVEMBER 11

I Samuel 16:1-13 and Ephesians 5:8-14

For the Lord sees not as man sees; man looks on the outward appearance, but the Lord looks on the heart. I SAMUEL 16:7

We are prone to look on the outward appearance, are we not? How many times have we been fooled into thinking someone to be something, only to find out on closer acquaintance that they did not measure up to our expectations! Or we may have had the uncomfortable experience of learning that people had expected of us what we could not be or could not produce, and that we turned out to be a disappointment to them.

God looks beyond the surface and sees what is inside. That is both reassuring and frightening. It is, of course, a healthy warning to us and a reminder that we are not fooling God. No matter how polite and correct we may be in our outward behavior, it is the heart, the real affection that God sees. That is why the psalmist prayed, "Search me . . . and see if there is any wicked way in me." For we do not always know what is in our own heart until God brings it to light.

Do we carry grudges in our hearts, feeling completely justified in our feelings toward someone who has wronged us? Do we allow our hearts to become cynical and hard because we resent the circumstances God has allowed to develop in our lives? It is very important not to harbor these negative feelings. They have a way of affecting us physically as well as spiritually.

Many of us have circumstances that, humanly speaking, are less than ideal. They can be an occasion of spiritual loss or spiritual gain, depending on what we let them do to our heart. I have known people who were outwardly blessed with wealth, favorable conditions, and physical health, but who were inwardly miserable and unhappy. I have also known people whose circumstances were full of trouble, inconvenience, even poverty—yet who maintained a courageous and sunny attitude in the midst of it. It was the heart that made the difference.

The God Who Remembers NOVEMBER 12

Exodus 32:1, 7-14 and Luke 15:1-10

Remember Abraham, Isaac and Israel, Thy servants. . . . And the
Lord repented of the evil he thought to do to his people.
EXODUS 32:13A, 14

This Old Testament passage is a vivid one—the people have
provoked the Lord beyond measure by turning to idols in
the short time since Moses received the Ten Commandments
on Mount Sinai. Here he is like an angry husband who has
been betrayed, or like an outraged father who cannot think
what to do next to his rebellious child. Who cannot feel the
grief and disappointment expressed here?

But God has bound himself with a sacred promise to
bring this people to the land where Abraham, Isaac and
Jacob lived. It is not for their glory but for God's glory that
he will keep his promise. Otherwise, Moses reminds him, the
nations will say that God has tricked the people in getting
them out of Egypt. And God then assures Moses that his
prayer has been heard and that he will indeed fulfill his
promise.

It is a part of God's great mercy that he has so bound
himself to us by sacred oath that he becomes obligated, as it
were, to deal with us. God remembers who you are and what
you are, and is working within the circumstances of your life
to bring his work in you to completion and perfection.

But see this: He also invites us to "remind" him of his
promise—not because he is going to forget, but because he
treats us seriously as persons. There is a verse in Isaiah which
appoints some of God's people as his "remembrancers."
"Upon your walls, O Jerusalem, I have set watchmen. . . .
You who put the Lord in remembrance, take no rest and give

him no rest until he establishes Jerusalem and makes it a praise in the earth" (Isaiah 62:6, 7). This is an invitation to be bold in our prayers, as Moses was bold before God in today's Old Testament reading.

We, too, can go to God with the assurance that he is a God who remembers his promises. He has given us many great and precious promises to encourage us to come to him in our need. If we meet his conditions of repentance and simple faith, he has bound himself by an eternal oath to forgive and bless us. How foolish we would be if we did not take him at his word!

The Promise of Completion   NOVEMBER 13

Philippians 1:1-11 and Luke 3:1-6

And I am sure that he who began a good work in
you will bring it to completion at the day
of Jesus Christ.   PHILIPPIANS 1:6

Most of us feel strongly that a task once started should be finished. My mother used to quote a little rhyme which went, "If a task is once begun, Never leave it till it's done. Be the labor great or small, Do it well, or not at all."

There is something particularly distressing about abandoned, half-finished jobs. Jesus talked about the importance of counting the cost before a project is begun, so that it can be completed to everyone's satisfaction.

We know that God counted the cost of saving us before his great work of redemption began, and was willing to go the distance. "God so loved the world that he gave his only begotten Son." He knew what the cost would be, and was willing to pay it.

Paul says with great assurance, "I am sure that he who began a good work in you will bring it to completion at the day of Jesus Christ." Has he begun that good work in you? Do you feel a need for such a Savior in your life, knowing that you cannot walk this path alone? Have you asked him to forgive you of your sins, and have you by simple faith put yourself and your future into his hands? Have you felt the stirring of faith, of hope, of trust in his mercy towards you? Have you felt an awakening desire to love him and to live as he would have you live? If so, he has begun a good work in you. If so, Paul says, "I am sure he will bring it to completion." God is faithful: nothing in our lives can hold back his saving power. His promises are sure, waiting for us to apply them to ourselves. Like a master workman, he is completing in us what he has undertaken, making, molding, chipping away, purifying us to be his and to enjoy him for ever.

Look at each day as an unfolding of that masterwork. Do not be discouraged at your failures, your "rough edges." He loves you. You are his. He has undertaken a great work, and, like a patient artist, he "will bring it to completion at the day of Jesus Christ."

Endurance   NOVEMBER 14

Hebrews 10:31-39 and Mark 13:14-23

For you have need of endurance, so that you may do the will of God and receive what is promised.   HEBREWS 10:36

A s we get older, I think perhaps we have greater appreciation for the things that have endured. We may have difficulty giving up an old hat or an old, comfortable pair of shoes! The lure of novelty is less powerful, the stability of things that last seems more important.

What all of us need—and what is available to all of us—is the strength and grace to endure. We do not have heroic faith, super-strong characters, or the courage of lions. Weak and needy as we are, there is a secret source of strength available this moment for whatever our need is. God has promised and God's work is faithful. He gives strength to those who flee to him for it. He never fails. We can endure because God's help is ever present, and past failures do not disqualify us from getting that present help.

God has all the strength it takes to help us endure whatever life is bringing at this moment. Whatever your particular circumstance, God is willing and able to help you "endure" and receive what is promised.

We do not have to wait for the life hereafter to inherit some of the promises of God, for he has said, "I will never leave you nor forsake you." And Jesus himself has told us, "Lo, I am with you always, even to the end of the world." We can press through, we can endure, and find his word fulfilled.

Made Like Us   NOVEMBER 15

Genesis 2:18-24 and Hebrews 2:9-18

Because he himself has suffered and been tempted, he is able to help those who are tempted.   HEBREWS 2:18

These are great passages from the Bible for today's reading. The first tells how God provided companionship for Adam in creating a helpmate for him. Just as he had created Adam out of his love and goodness, desiring to share life with this creature made in his own image, he now completes the creative act by making a second person—so that creation becomes complete: male and female. God bestows a dignity and honor on this bit of clay into which he has breathed the breath of life, calling us his own children and enabling humanity to share in his creative work. It is an honor we have often abused and distorted. Much of our creativity has been turned in wrong directions, and we have certainly often used our relations with our fellow human beings in destructive rather than constructive ways.

The writer of Hebrews deals with the reality of human life as it exists in the present—and he uses such terms as "fear of death," "bondage," and "suffering." What started out so beautifully and hopefully in the Garden of Eden was soon turned into a very different picture when sin and alienation from God entered the picture. And that process of alienation and separation from our Creator has continued right down to our own lives, so that we know personally what it means to live in the fear of death, in bondage to evil thoughts and habits, and what it means to suffer as a result of our own wrong decisions and those of others.

This is what makes the gospel such welcome news. "We see Jesus," says the writer. "We see Jesus," and suddenly things begin to change. Here is hope for our despair, help for our need, healing for our wounds.

Can he help you and me? "Because he himself was tempted, he is able to help . . . ." Stop there and fill in the blank with your own situation. He is able to help you. That is where your faith and mine lay hold on his ableness, his power to help us. Today, whatever temptation assails you— to despair, to feel sorry for yourself, to say or do wrong—he can help you and will help you if you truly want him to. Don't miss the blessing!

Receiving Good News   NOVEMBER 16

Nehemiah 8:2-12 and Luke 4:14-21

The Spirit of the Lord is upon me, because he has anointed me to preach good news to the poor. LUKE 4:18A

The Scriptures present only one antidote for bad news, and that is the Good News! Can you remember where you were and what you were doing on V-J Day? V-E Day? How about the day John Glenn flew into space, or the day Neil Armstrong took his "small step" on the moon? Good news has a way of sticking in our minds and hearts.

When Jesus stood before the citizens of Nazareth, he brought to them the best news their hearts could ever hope to receive: "He has anointed me to preach good news." The Good News of God's love is the only lasting antidote for the bitter taste of bad news. And, just as bad news is a natural part of this world's order, so Good News is the most natural and pervasive thing in the kingdom of God. As children of God, we have access to it each and every day.

> God so loved the world. . . . John 3:16
> All things work together for good. . . . Romans 8:28
> Nothing can separate us from the love of God. . . .
>   Romans 8:39
> Thanks be to God, who gives us the victory. . . .
>   I Corinthians 15:57

When the Hebrews listened to Ezra reading from the book of the law, they were not sure at first what kind of news they were hearing. But soon they went their way "to eat and drink . . . and to make great rejoicing, because they had understood the words that were declared to them" (Nehemiah 8:12). They had received good news! We have received it, too.

Let Not Your Heart Be Troubled NOVEMBER 17

Psalm 66:8-20 and John 14:15-31

Peace I leave with you, my peace I give unto you; not as the world gives do I give to you. Let not your hearts be troubled, neither let them be afraid. JOHN 14:27

Jesus utters these familiar words twice in this chapter (John 14:1 and 27). They were spoken to a confused and worried group of men on the very night Jesus was betrayed by Judas and seized by the soldiers in the Garden of Gethsemane.

Jesus could concentrate on the needs of his disciples, knowing that their faith would soon be sorely tested, because he had fully committed himself to carrying out the Father's will, no matter what. It is wrong to think of Jesus' obedience as something easy and automatic, because that would make light of it. The Book of Hebrews tells us that he was in every respect "tempted as we are, yet without sinning." And it adds, "Because he himself has suffered and been tempted, he is able to help those who are tempted" (Hebrews 2:18).

These words of Jesus, "Let not your hearts be troubled," are both an invitation and a command. They are an invitation to move into a new realm of reality. Jesus knows how easy it is to give in to fear. When we are confronted with bad news, or when we get sick, or when something bad happens to someone dear to us, our natural reaction is fear.

Jesus invites us to look at such things through the eye of faith by the help of the Comforter, the Counselor, the Holy Spirit. And the secret of the Christian is that there is an invisible source of strength and comfort available in all our needs. The Lord would never have invited us not to let our hearts be troubled if he was not going to provide a way through troublesome places.

But this is more than an invitation. It is a command. Your fear and mine, your worry and mine—these do not honor God nor give him glory. We can deal with them by confessing our lack of faith and our lack of thankfulness for past mercies. "Lord, I am afraid, and I know that this means I am not trusting you as I should. You have always been faithful, and I'm sorry for my lack of faith. Forgive me for not trusting you, and change my heart. I choose to believe that you are working to bring good out of this. Nothing is greater than your love and nothing can separate me from it. Amen."

The Presence   NOVEMBER 18

Exodus 19:16-24 and Matthew 18:15-20

For where two or three are gathered in my name, there am I in the midst of them. MATTHEW 18:20

Today's text reminds us that we find God's presence in company with others. "Where two or three are gathered in my name." In the preceding verse Jesus was talking about our need to agree in prayer in order to strengthen our prayer requests. We are part of a company—the Church, the Body of Christ.

We make a mistake, however, if we think of the "two or three" as being simply gathered in a service of some kind. What Jesus is talking about can occur in our homes, where two or three family members are sharing some deep concern together. It might be when you and a friend talk about the most ordinary things, when your heart is warmed to love, to care, to send up a little silent prayer to God for his or her need. Jesus says that when these little meetings take place, "There am I in the midst of them."

Even when you are reading these words, that same promise applies. For I pray for each one of you, that in some way, quite beyond our knowledge or understanding, we become sharers of his company. And when you read your Bible, you are in company with the apostles, the martyrs, the saints, the faithful of all ages.

In Psalm 149 we read that "the Lord takes pleasure in his people." He calls us to allow others into our lives, because it is through them that we are able to catch new glimpses of him and a better understanding of ourselves. We receive more of what Christ has for us through others than we can receive without them. That is what he is talking about as he says, "Where two or three are gathered in my name, there am I in the midst of them." It is his promise and his provision. What a comfort to know that he is present.

Pleasant Boundaries   NOVEMBER 19

Psalm 16 and Luke 7:36-50

The [boundary] lines have fallen for me in pleasant places;
yea, I have a goodly heritage.   PSALM 16:6

This verse has intrigued me for a long time. Look at your circumstances. Trace the workings of God in your life. Look back across the years—few or many—and see the Hand at work, guiding, steering, shaping, correcting. "The lines have fallen for me in pleasant places."

There is no denying that some of us have painful memories. Real wrongs may have been inflicted on us. There is no use to "white wash" the situations and say, "People didn't know better."

But we can choose to wrap the drapery of self-pity around us and charge ourselves with the role of "chief victim." Or we can begin to seek a better way. Out of the darkest time of evil, the most unmitigated horror, we do have a choice: bitterness or forgiveness. If we choose forgiveness, we will not find it comes easily. It is a costly gift, and may strip us of some of our dearest qualities: superiority and self-righteousness. But if we desire it, knowing that God has commanded it and that he will make it possible—then it will be ours.

Surely I have a goodly heritage. It wasn't all pleasant. It wasn't all that I would have wanted it to be. It was flawed by the human condition: my own and that of others. But God is greater than our flaws. He has not forgotten his own, and he will not forget us.

When Courage Fails   NOVEMBER 20

I Kings 19:1-8, Galatians 2:15-21 and Luke 7:36-8:3

*Then [Elijah] was afraid, and he arose and went for his life . . .
and came and sat under a broom tree; and he asked that he
might die, saying, "It is enough . . . ."*   I KINGS 19:3A, 4B

There is hardly a story anywhere more dramatic and exciting than the story of Elijah and the priests of Baal in their showdown on the top of Mount Carmel. A single, faithful servant of God pitted against the hosts of Baal, with the Queen herself egging on her protégés, the alien priests of a foreign god. Everything that Israel was called to be and stand for was at stake.

And then came the showdown itself. First, Elijah told the priests of Baal to "do their things." And they prepared their sacrifices, placed them on the altar, did their religious rituals and waited to see what would happen. But when nothing happened, they began to grow increasingly frightened and even desperate—cutting themselves with swords and lances. Then, when it was time for the evening sacrifice, Elijah prayed a simple, beautiful prayer, and fire fell from heaven consuming everything. And the people cried, "The Lord, he is God!"

But everyone was not pleased. Queen Jezebel sent Elijah a little note: "May the gods do even more to me than you did to my priests if I don't have your neck by this time tomorrow." The great hero, Elijah, who had just slain 450 priests, "arose and went for his life."

We sometimes find ourselves in that place. We may have come through a great trial. Faith may have sustained us, God was with us, and grace was upon us. And then our courage fails. But God is still there with us, supplying needed strength. So when courage fails us, and we want to give up, remember that others, too, feel this way and have felt this way—even great heroes like Elijah. God knows and understands—and will supply needed strength for that situation, too.

Be Reconciled NOVEMBER 21

I Corinthians 3:1-9 and Matthew 5:21-37

If you are offering your gift at the altar, and there remember that
your brother has something against you, leave your gift there
before the altar and go; first be reconciled to your brother, and
then come and offer your gift. MATTHEW 5:23, 24

It is easier to remember the things we hold against others than to think of what they may hold against us. But Jesus is saying something vitally important to us: He is more interested in our being reconciled with those we have hurt than he is with the gifts we offer him.

Then there are the harder ones. The hasty, unkind word said in anger, the spiteful look, the sullen withdrawal that left its own message. Silences can be very cruel. I expect that we all have our little catalog of hurts and resentments and unforgivenesses that we need to look at. As we grow older, the need for reconciliation is even more urgent. We should not allow life to run out with bitterness still alive in our hearts.

Today, if there is someone with whom you need to be reconciled, do not delay. Time is precious. God's mercy is so great that it encompasses the "wrong ones" on both sides of the question. Let us be willing to be reconciled, and especially willing to ask forgiveness where we have hurt others.

Loving One Another NOVEMBER 22

I John 4:11-16 and John 17:11-19

Beloved, if God so loved us, we also ought to love one another.
I JOHN 4:11

Today's texts spotlight God's great love to us in our Lord and Savior, Jesus Christ, and his desire that we love one another with the same kind of love. What kind of love was it?

First, it was a "going before" kind of love. He loved us before we loved him. His love for us was not conditioned on our love for him. God's love—not ours—is primary. If our relationship with God depended on our love, we would have a very weak foundation, one that shifts with moods. Sometimes we love him, to be sure. But at other times we forget him. Sometimes we are angry at him or jealous of him, because he is God and we are not! But that "going before" kind of love did not ask our permission to love us. When we awakened to it, it was already there—just as our parents' love preceded our love for them. That is the great wonder of God's love.

Second, the love we receive in Jesus is a forgiving love. I heard someone say recently that the most important thing in our life of faith is to forgive. Our human nature finds it very hard to forgive real wrong. We may overlook or excuse little things, but when something is done that truly wounds us, we find the cost of forgiving very high indeed. The love we find in Jesus does not make light of wrong. It shows that forgiveness even costs God—so the mystery of the cross always stands to show how much it cost God, yet how far his love is willing to go to offer it freely.

Third, the love we received in Jesus doesn't quit.

Rejection of God does not turn off his love. If we are going to love as God loves, we will have to love through rejection, betrayal, neglect, indifference—all the things that happen in imperfect relationships. Love that lasts—and lasts—and lasts: that is the kind of love God shows us.

For this kind of love to grow in our hearts, there is another kind of love that has to die and be weeded out—love of self, love of having our own way, wanting people to love and serve us. For God's love to grow, we must make room. It's there, in us, for the "Holy Spirit has shed it abroad in our hearts." And every day, no matter what our circumstances, we have a choice to make—to let the old selfish "love" rule, or to make room for the kind of love that God has planted in us.

Distress and Deliverance NOVEMBER 23

Psalm 107 and John 21:1-19

Then they cried to the Lord in their trouble, and he delivered them from their distress. PSALM 107:6
[ALSO PSALM 107:13 AND 19]

Here we have the pattern of the history of Israel in its relation with God. And here we have the pattern of our relationship with the same God.

Some wandered. That was the way the psalmist described the condition of the first group about which he is singing. Some wandered in desert wastes. That image has been continued through the centuries as an apt description of our life before we come to kneel in submissive faith and obedience before the Lord.

Our wanderings may not have been as dramatic as those of the prodigal son, but they were enough to land us in "desert wastes," the futile and fruitless point at which we knew we were in trouble.

"Some sat in darkness . . . prisoners in affliction. . . ." Not wandering at all, but imprisoned in prisons of our own making! It was not only the prodigal son who would not be controlled, but the elder son as well, who despised his father's generosity and thereby built a prison of self-righteousness and hate for himself. The constriction of our prisons brings us to cry to the Lord for deliverance. Then, we are told, "He delivered them from their distress; he brought them out of darkness and gloom, and broke their bonds asunder." A triple deliverance!

Here each one of us could perhaps add our personal testimony of how God's deliverance has worked and how it continues to work. In spite of all our good intentions, we still find ourselves in situations where there is nothing to do but to cry to the Lord in our trouble. And his ear is still open to the cry of his children. We do not have to allow any circumstance to keep us long in the prison house of darkness or the desert wastes of our wandering hearts. We have a God who hears and who helps. He is "a very present help in time of need."

Thirsting and Drinking NOVEMBER 24

Isaiah 55:1-9 and I Corinthians 10:1-13

Ho, every one who thirsts, come to the waters; and he who has no money, come, buy and eat! Come, buy wine and milk without honey and without price. ISAIAH 55:1

Thirst alerts us to a basic human need: the need for water. Without it, we soon perish. Thirst, then, is a part of our built-in safety system to compel us to seek "the water of life." The prophet is talking about another thirst: a thirst for God. His call is to those who feel dissatisfied with life without God. The psalmist answers this call with the words, "My soul thirsts for God, for the living God" (Psalm 42:2). Someone has said that every human being has within him or her "a God-shaped blank," meaning that without God we are not complete. St. Augustine said, "Our hearts are restless until they rest in thee."

But we may have lived long ignoring this thirst. So the prophet asked us, "Why do you spend your money for that which cannot satisfy?" Why, in other words, do we spend our interest, our energy and our time on things that can provide only a momentary distraction, while neglecting the thing we most need? It's a question worth pondering at any point in our lives.

"Seek the Lord while he may be found," says our Scripture. "Call upon him while he is near." There are moments, times and seasons when we feel the tug of the Spirit more strongly than at other times. These special times, when in the quiet of our heart we hear or feel a whispered word, are indications that God is near, that he is seeking us, even as he invites us to seek him. "Call upon him while he is near."

The truth is, I think, that these words are written for those who thirst, and who want to have a stronger faith in God. We are sojourners together in a walk of faith, and we need to encourage one another, as the prophet does, to seek and find, and to drink of the water of life which God offers to "everyone who thirsts."

O Taste and See   NOVEMBER 25

Psalm 34 and Ephesians 4:1-6

O taste and see that the Lord is good! Happy is the man who takes refuge in him! PSALM 34:8

What do you suppose the psalmist is saying when he invites us to "taste and see that the Lord is good"? Have you ever put something into your mouth and found an unpleasant surprise awaiting you? When I was very young, I dipped something into a can of lye and put it on my tongue. Fortunately my grandmother was near and washed it out immediately, but I carry the scar to this day. A very unpleasant surprise! Some things disappoint us. Some even carry destruction with them. So it pays to be careful what we "taste."

The same is true of life. Some people choose to "taste" experiences which are laden with destruction. Think of the drug users and the sad end that awaits them. Some people choose wrong ways of living and wreak unhappiness on themselves and their families. Not so those who choose to believe in Jesus Christ and follow him. He said, "Those who come to me shall not hunger and those who believe in me shall never thirst." He does not ask us to believe in fantasies and unrealities. He is prepared to stand behind his promises.

All of us have our share in the sweetness of life and the bitterness of it. All of us have disappointments and griefs that we have to bear. But how blessed are those who have tasted and who know that the Lord is good! How blessed are those who take refuge in him.

Abundant Life   NOVEMBER 26

Psalm 23 and John 10:1-10

I came that they may have life and have it abundantly.
JOHN 10:10B

These words are Jesus' own statement about the intent and purpose of his life. From the time he became conscious of who he was, he was committed to that single purpose. It was the fulfillment of the Father's will for him, for he was sent into the world, "not to condemn the world, but that the world might be saved through him" (John 3:17).

How do you understand those words "abundant life"? I have known people who "had everything" and were miserable. You wouldn't say they had abundant life, though they had everything in abundance. It seems, if anything, that being abundantly blessed in material wealth presents even more problems to some people. Where is the secret, and what is this abundant life Jesus came to give?

Abundant life is a gift of love. It is knowing that we are loved, and finding the ability to love others "in spite of ourselves." Jesus came to show us that God cares about us more than we can ever imagine; the cross demonstrates that God goes all the way with his love. So we are invited into a life of being loved supremely and of becoming loving persons. We are recipients of the love of those around us, of God's love through them. Look around you at the abundance of love which the Father has bestowed on you!

Abundant life is a life of joy. If you are a child of God and believe in Jesus Christ, God dwells within your spirit, and there should be and can be a deep sense of joy that carries us through the griefs and trials we must all face. The Scripture says that Jesus, "for the joy that was set before him, endured the cross, making light of its disgrace" (Hebrews 12:3, NEB).

Abundant life is a life of peace. Paul speaks of "the peace of God which passes all understanding," and surely his peace is that. The saints and martyrs have given testimony to it, and we ourselves may have experienced it in some especially difficult time.

If you want these qualities in greater abundance in your life, seek for them from the giver of all good, the One who came that we might have life and have it abundantly, even Jesus Christ our Lord. He will not fail.

Faith's Fair Vision   NOVEMBER 27

Psalm 86 and Romans 8:18-25

In this hope we were saved.   ROMANS 8:24

Life has a lot of "nights." All of us have those times when the lights not only seem dim, but seem to have gone out completely. A dear friend of mine recently went through that kind of "dark night of the soul." His son's wife died, completing a kind of strange cycle in which every one of his children had experienced some kind of tragic loss. This experience took its toll on my friend, and he found himself angry at God—so angry, in fact, that he had to lay aside his work for a time and go away so that he could wrestle with God about the whole thing. The night was dark, and he needed to know that God was not playing tricks on him.

Do you have something you could call "faith's fair vision?" However beautiful the present world is (and it is truly a beautiful, glorious creation), it is not the last word. It is a mortal, passing world. And our "faith's fair vision" must look beyond it. We cannot afford to let our vision be limited to this brief life here on earth. God made us for more than that. He made us, as the old catechism says, "To adore him and enjoy him forever."

John Bunyan, in his great spiritual allegory, *The Pilgrim's Progress*, pictures Christian and Hopeful, the two pilgrims, as arriving at "the country of Beulah, whose air was very sweet and pleasant. Here they heard continually the singing of birds and saw every day the flowers appear in the earth, and heard the voice of the turtle-dove in the land. In this country the sun shines night and day. Here they were within sight of the City to which they were going, and here they met some of its inhabitants, because it was upon the borders of heaven." That is the way Bunyan pictures that state of life when we have fought many battles—won some and lost some, but have continued on the way of faith, keeping our eye ever forward to where God is leading us. It is so very important not to lose sight of that when the night comes.

Paul says simply, "In this hope we are saved." Do not let go "faith's fair vision," and keep hold on the hope that is set before us.

Twelve Baskets Full   NOVEMBER 28

Romans 8:31-39 and Matthew 14:13-21

And they all ate and were satisfied. And they took up twelve baskets full of the broken pieces left over.   MATTHEW 14:20

The main point of this story is that through this miracle God provided food for 5,000 people, and that there was such an overabundance that twelve baskets full were taken up for later use! Talk about the generosity of God!

"They all ate and were satisfied," says the evangelist. What does that say to us now, where we are? Before that miracle the people were hungry and the disciples were perplexed. "This is a lonely place," they said. "The day is over. Send the crowds away to go into the villages and buy food for themselves." The disciples looked at that crowd and concluded, very logically, that there were too many people, and the need was too great. The disciples knew that they didn't have what was needed to satisfy the people. Yet at that very point, Jesus said, "You give them something to eat!" But the only thing they could come up with was a little meal of five biscuit-like loaves and two fish.

What Jesus did then was to take that insufficient lunch and turn it into a satisfying banquet. And that is a picture of what he does with whatever we give him. He transforms it. He turns it into something more than it was when we had it. He makes it into something that brings refreshment, blessing and life to others. In order to have that happen, though, we have to turn it over to him—truly give it to him. Whatever it is that we have—talent, personality, the gift of being friendly with others, stories that we might remember from our past which could bless others—whatever it is, if it is turned over to him, it can become more than we think or dare hope.

We all do want to bring blessing and joy to others, do we not? It is very satisfying and fulfilling to see something we have done, or said or made, cause another person's face to light up with joy. That is what Jesus does with what we offer and truly turn over to him.

For Us

Romans 4:13-25 and Mark 8:31-38

It will be reckoned to us who believe in him that raised from the dead Jesus our Lord, who was put to death for our trespasses and raised for our justification. ROMANS 4:24, 25

Jesus' whole life was a journey from Bethlehem to Calvary. It is very clear that he could have chosen another way, but he chose the way laid out for him by his Father in heaven. He came for us. His mission on earth was to seek and save the lost. He talked about lost sheep, lost coins, and a lost son. But he never lost sight of what he had come to do. In today's Gospel reading, he reminds his disciples that he would have to suffer many things. He was trying to prepare them for what lay ahead.

It was not good news to any of them. The disciples were looking for victory, not suffering. They were like us, wanting things to be successful, and here Jesus was talking about dying. They didn't understand, and indeed, did not understand until after it was over. Only then did they remember and begin to perceive the depth of Jesus' love and care.

Jesus talks about trying to save our lives and losing them in the process, and about losing our lives for his sake and saving them. This is a paradox—something that seems to contradict itself but really doesn't. It is a truth we find as we live, that if we cling to life and try to save it, it slips out of our hands. But if we give it away to God, he gives it back to us in renewed hope and strength. Death does not have to be the end of everything. Death is a reality to be faced, but if we have given our lives to God, then it can only be a time of change from one form of life to another.

This is all true whether we accept it or not. Jesus has

paid the price for us. He has come with love and healing. He is still in the saving business, and he still seeks the lost sheep and the lost son. In other words, he still seeks us.

Whatever You Do　　　　　　　NOVEMBER 30

Ecclesiastes 1:12-14, 2:18-23 and Colossians 3:13-21

And whatever you do, in word or deed, do everything in the name of the Lord Jesus, giving thanks to God the Father through him. COLOSSIANS 3:17

The Book of Ecclesiastes is in many ways a strange book. The writer seems to think that, when all is said and done, life is vain. He goes on in these early verses to tell how he had tried everything, and still found his life empty. That, of course, is what vanity means—emptiness. The world cannot fill what it was never created to fill. Someone has observed that we have a "God-shaped blank" within us that only God can fill.

Too many people try to fill that aching void, that emptiness which cries out for God, with things of the world. And the world always betrays them, because it cannot satisfy our thirst for God. In the Gospel of Luke, Jesus tells about a successful farmer who forgot his soul in the process of conducting his business. He got so wrapped up in bigger fields, bigger crops and bigger barns that God was crowded out entirely. Jesus says that just when everything was looking so rosy for the future, God spoke and called the man a fool. We were made for something more than building bigger barns and bigger businesses. We have business with our Creator!

In today's Epistle to the Colossians, Paul gives us the secret of being satisfied. He does not guarantee that everything will be just the way we want it. Paul knew what it was to suffer hunger and need, rejection by family and friends, misunderstanding even from his fellow Christians, and in addition to that, a bodily affliction which did not get healed. So he had his share of difficulties. But he says, "Whatever you do, in word or deed, do everything in the name of the Lord Jesus, giving thanks to God the Father through him." And that, I believe, is the key, the way to turn things in a different direction, the way out of emptiness and bitterness, the way to inner fulfillment: giving thanks, cultivating a grateful heart.

When we take our life as coming from Christ—the good and the bad—and offer it back to him the best way we can, our inner attitude begins to align itself with God's peace. When we stop fighting our circumstances and say, "Father, I do not understand all the 'why's' but I choose to trust you and thank you for being with me in this," clouds part and the warmth of his love begins to penetrate our inner darkness. Try it. He is our peace, and he wants to share that peace and fulfillment with us all our days.

DECEMBER

Everlasting Arms

*Now the dwelling of God is
with men, and he will live with
them. They will be his people,
and God himself will be with
them and be their God. He
will wipe every tear from their
eyes. There will be no more
death or mourning or crying or
pain, for the old order of things
has passed away.*

REVELATION 21:3B (NIV)

"In Him Will I Trust"
-Psalm 91:2b

As I waited for the phone call from the doctor, I prayed and prayed fervently. I felt the Lord said to me, "My grace is sufficient for this day. Walk in it!" And then with one telephone call, my world turned from right side up to upside down. The doctor's words, "Your husband's aorta has ruptured," are still emblazoned on my memory as though it was yesterday.

As we drove to the hospital where he was being prepared for a helicopter flight to Boston to undergo open-heart surgery, my mind raced with a multitude of thoughts and feelings. "I am not ready to be a widow" was one of the first. But that early morning word about walking in his grace was the underlying support, as I began a long walk through the anxiety-riddled, heart-clutching fear that comes when you face losing someone you love.

Driving to Boston with my family, I looked up and saw the helicopter taking Zack to Boston. I thought I must be dreaming. This can't really be happening. How can he be up in the air fighting for his life, and I be down here making what would normally be a routine drive to Boston? For a person who has always tried to stay in control of every situation, this was the ultimate in being out of control. There was nothing I could do but ride on. I began to feel like a child, a very frightened child, but nonetheless a child who needed as never before to trust in his sufficient grace. I was being carried where I did not wish to go, but go I must.

Throughout my life, my faith has been tried and tested in small and large ways and always God has been faithful to carry me through whatever he asked, but this test seemed too large. I was not sure I had any faith at all for this one. It was a shock to realized that I was not what I thought I was. I moved as though in a dream. When my children suggested I eat, make a phone call, take a break, I obeyed without argument or question. This was a unique experience for all of us! I only wish I might have stayed so yielded and submissive.

Throughout these days, the prayers and support of family and friends became a lifeline and undergirding that is hard to describe, but oh, so real. I felt strength that wasn't my own. I had heard of the prayers of the saints, but now I knew personally what those prayers provided.

His grace did carry us through the first surgery, which saved Zack's life but did not totally correct the damage. More was to follow. We returned home with grateful hearts, praising God for his love, mercy and goodness, determined to never fall short of the mark again. For once, priorities were in the right order.

As Zack's strength and health began to return, so did my impatience and irritation with insignificant things. He was angry that he could not do what he used to do, and I was angry that he could not do what he used to do—for me! It is with shame that I make this confession, but also with a new maturity, acknowledging my absolute total need to keep Jesus first and foremost in my life.

Three months later, we returned to Brigham and Women's Hospital in Boston for replacement of a dissected carotid artery and more lessons. Once again, I experienced the same fears and anxieties, and once again the same grace. Upon returning home, the same failings. I felt like a yo-yo being whipped around by my emotions . . . one day up, another day down. Discouragement hit and bottomed out, but when hope and encouragement arrived in the form of good news, all things were possible again.

After this second surgery, I took an adamant position of "no more." I was totally unwilling to subject Zack to further torture. How little I know about the workings of God. When a call came explaining the seriousness of my husband's continuing condition and the necessity for yet another operation, my heart melted into a small lump of softened clay, with the fight gone. One month later, we were on our way to Boston for the third round. And again eight months later, we faced the fourth and what was to be the final operation for the replacement of additional sections of Zack's dissected aorta.

Each surgery was a fresh experience of facing who I am and accepting my own humanity . . . one who must constantly, each and every day, stay closely connected to the One who is the source of salvation, grace and forgiveness. I learned that I am like a barometer, going up and down spiritually with changes in the atmosphere. When I am with him and in him, I am at peace. When I forget and wander away, I become fearful, angry, restless, anxious, and rebellious. For me, it is as simple as that. "His grace is sufficient for this day. Walk in it."

Mary Ann Jamison

Amazing Grace! DECEMBER 1

Psalm 89:20-37 and Ephesians 2:1-10

For by grace you have been saved through faith, and this is not your own doing; it is the gift of God—not because of works, lest any man should boast. EPHESIANS 2:8, 9

It seems that this old gospel hymn, "Amazing Grace," is one of the most popular religious songs in the whole world. As most of us know, it was written by John Newton, the former slave trader who had been converted and became a minister of the Church of England and an accomplished hymn writer. But this hymn expressed his inward journey from total rebellion and shame. There are some very important thoughts that tie in with our text.

First, we need to remember that grace is, by its very definition, something given, not earned. We do not receive God's grace because we deserve it. Rather, it is because we do not deserve it that it is "grace." Otherwise, we would just be rewarded for earning God's favor. This is a very hard concept for most of us, because we have tried to prove that we are worthy. The gospel tells us that we don't have to prove that. God loves us as we are, and he does not wait for us to become "worthy" in that sense. In fact, if we believe what he tells us in the Bible, we can never earn his favor, and we don't have to! We already have it!

John Newton, however, says that it was grace that taught his heart to fear. Without the fear of the Lord, there is no possibility of change. Newton had virtually "sold" himself in his life of sin. And he realized that if God's grace had not brought fear in his heart, he would have continued headlong in that path right to death. Fear keeps us from "going over the cliff," so to speak. It stops us in our tracks and makes us consider: Where am I heading? Is this what life is all about? Do I want to live out my life without God and face an eternity without him? Or am I created for something else? That kind of godly fear brings us very near to faith.

Then Newton goes on to say, "grace my fear relieved." The Holy Spirit quickens our consciences and tells us that we need to repent. Then he points us to Jesus, the forgiving Savior, who forgives our sins and relieves our fears. We have peace with God because we have not hidden the dark secrets of our thoughts from God. We have owned up to them, and have received the miracle of forgiveness of our sins. Sins are not just getting drunk, stealing, killing or being unfaithful. Sins also involve our selfish thoughts, even our faithless fears. And when we allow God to point them out, repent of them, and find his loving, merciful forgiveness, we know that it is his grace operating in our lives.

It is all a gift. No wages, no merits. Just the gracious gift of a gracious God who loves us and wants us to be in harmony with him. What more could we ask or desire?

And Then You Shall Know . . . DECEMBER 2

Exodus 16:2-15 and Matthew 15:21-28

At twilight you shall eat flesh, and in the morning you shall be filled with bread; then you shall know that I am the Lord your God. EXODUS 16:12B

The people of Israel were embarked on a very great adventure. They had been persuaded to leave the safety of their slave-life in Egypt, to venture forth to a land they had heard about but had never seen. Moses, their leader, assured them that God was leading them forth into undreamed-of freedom. God was not new to them, for they had been taught from childhood about him.

But things were not that simple! They were not prepared for all that awaited them on their journey to the Promised Land. Very soon they became discouraged, and began to cry out, "Would that we had died by the hand of the Lord in Egypt!"

Are we not like them? How easy it is to forget how difficult situations were in the past, and begin to romanticize our memories, longing for something that never was! God was patient with the Israelites and he is patient with us.

God intends that we shall learn to trust him more, learn more fully who he is. Knowing him is not something that comes from books. It is something that comes through all our experiences, good and bad, happy and sad. The Israelites were given quail to eat because they had murmured against God, and they were given manna, the bread of heaven, because God loved them. The first made them sick and the second gave them strength. In both cases, they were to learn to know "that I am the Lord."

Think of how God has blessed you and provided for you when you were unable to provide for yourself. He has always been with you and is still with you each day, using all the things that happen to help you come to know him more fully. He always gives us grace to accept whatever the day brings. So the whole story of your life and mine, of our journey from the slavery of self to the Promised Land of freedom, is a story of coming to know him, in the deepest part of our being, and to know him better and better.

The Mystery of Suffering   DECEMBER 3

Hebrews 5:5-10 and John 12:20-33

Although he (Jesus) was a Son, he learned obedience through
what he suffered; and being made perfect he became the source
of eternal salvation to all who obey him.   HEBREWS 5:8, 9

Every living person suffers. No one escapes this strange
and mysterious part of our human existence. Sometimes
we are called on to endure physical pain or discomfort—and
that is certainly suffering of a kind. Or, we may suffer hurts
inflicted by others, intentionally or unintentionally. We suffer from what rises up out of our own nature. We suffer from
the loss of people we love—friends and family. We suffer
from fears, worries and anxieties.

The Bible is of great help in facing life as it is. The Bible
recognizes that the result of human sin has made suffering
inevitable. It was into our world that Jesus came. He was the
Son of God, and yet, in order to reach us in our many needs,
he became one of us, the Son of Mary. And our text says,
"He was made perfect through what he suffered." So, having experienced the same kinds of suffering we face, he is
able to meet us right where we need him.

We believe that somehow, in God's eternal wisdom, suffering is not useless, that it is not an accident that it happens
to us, and that it is not to be thrown away. Therefore, do not
let your suffering plunge you into self pity. If you find yourself there, pray earnestly for help in getting out of the pit.

Second, offer your suffering up to God. "Father, I do not
understand this, but I choose to trust you. I offer it up to
you." Two of my friends are experiencing much inner healing through serious suffering, so I can see God's purpose
being fulfilled, even as I pray for their physical healing.

Finally, believe that he knows how much you can bear,

and never allows you to suffer more than he gives you grace to bear it. Remember that he loves you and is with you in it all.

Pressing On   DECEMBER 4

Psalm 8 and Philippians 3:12-21

I press on to make it my own, because Christ Jesus has made me his own.   PHILIPPIANS 3:12B

We all know what it means to "press on." It has to do with going on when we are tired, when the going gets tough, when we would rather relax. It is the language of the soldier on march, whose feet are tired and whose load is heavy, who cannot afford to sit down and rest by the way. He must press on.

In our physical, earthly life—as we have experienced many times in carrying on our duties—we know that pressing on is a necessary part of living a responsible, meaningful life. So it is in our spiritual life. To give up, to let little doubts or fears or failures discourage us so that we decide it isn't worth it all, is the height of foolishness. Pressing on is as necessary in the realm of faith and the spirit as it is in mountain climbing or raising a family.

Paul adds another reason: "Because Christ Jesus has made me his own." For Paul that was enough. To know that somehow in the infinite mercy and goodness of God, Jesus Christ had reached out and made Paul one of his, had claimed him for himself, was enough to steel his nerve for all that life could throw at him. Most of us will not be called on to suffer as Paul did. But "there is much to suffer" and "there is much to dare" for every one of us. How wonderful it is when those sufferings come, to be strengthened and comforted by knowing that Jesus loves us, claims us, and even now is supplying us with grace to "press on." It is enough. It is enough. Thanks be to God!

But He Gives More Grace   DECEMBER 5

James 3:16-4:6 and Mark 9:30-37

But he gives more grace; therefore it says, "God opposes the proud, but gives grace to the humble."   JAMES 4:6

The word "grace" is a most interesting one. It is akin to "graceful" and "gracious" and "grateful" and, according to the dictionary, comes from the Latin word meaning "beloved, dear." So put them all together, and we begin to get a picture of what God is saying to us in this little verse, "But he gives more grace."

What it says to me is that, in spite of who I am, and all the things about myself that I would like to be different, there is the grace of God, the undeserved love and favor of God, which is mine. "Grace that is greater than all our sins," as the old gospel song puts it. What an encouragement that is when we're feeling particularly bad about ourselves.

Then it says that if I choose to look at my present life, in spite of the things I don't like, the conditions I cannot change, I can choose to be more grace-ful by being more grateful. If I allow the grace that comes from God to enter my inmost heart, others will see a graceful quality that is not natural to me, and they will respond to it. So even if outward conditions cannot change, the atmosphere around me and my relationships will change—for the better. Because God gives more grace.

Wages and Gifts DECEMBER 6

Ezekiel 37:1-3, 11-14 and Romans 6:16-23

For the wages of sin is death, but the free gift of God is eternal life in Christ Jesus our Lord. ROMANS 6:23

It seems to be a human tendency to keep saying we "deserve" this or that. We want to be praised and paid for our good thoughts and good actions.

That's the way many of Christians look at their relationship with God. Life is a matter of earning rewards and keeping record.

Paul talks about this whole way of approaching God in this chapter of Romans. First, he establishes that if it is a simple matter of wages, since we are all sinners, our wages will be death. But once we know our real condition before God, we change our cry from what we deserve to what we need. We need forgiveness. We need peace with God. We cannot earn that, no matter how hard we try, because of who we are. So Paul bids us to abandon our demand to "get paid."

The essence of the gospel is the good news that Christ came for the undeserving. He came to us in our need, in our inability to change ourselves, and first acquainted us with our real condition. He himself lived among us and gave up his life so that we might have forgiveness. When we are willing to receive it, he gives us eternal life as a free gift.

Our relationship with the Lord is based on that gift.

We've all earned our wages—just being who we are and acting the way we all do. But we have all been given that wonderful gift, a gift that grows more precious as the years go by. Have you accepted his gift in your own heart?

How Can We Know the Way?   DECEMBER 7

Psalm 31:1-8 and John 14:1-14

Thomas said to him, "Lord, we do not know where you are going; how can we know the way?" JOHN 14:5

Thomas has been called "the doubter." He did not hesitate to blurt out his lack of understanding when Jesus was teaching. His was what we might call "a practical turn of mind." He reasoned that you could not know the way unless you knew where you were going. Jesus had spoken many times to this little group about where he had come from and where he was going.

But they had not heard him—not really. Their own ideas about what he was to do were completely different. Like us, they wanted a victorious Leader who would save them from suffering, sorrow, and all the bad things of life.

What this says to us is that Jesus does not offer a cheap, easy way of life. He shows us a way, instead, through the difficulties, disappointments and setbacks of life. God did not spare his own dearly beloved Son the pain and suffering of the cross. Why? Because through that suffering God would reconcile us to himself. So why does he allow us to suffer, to be disappointed, to face trials and hardships? Because through them we are trained and chastened, weaned from insisting on our own way, and made more ready to live as his children in his eternal kingdom.

Jesus could say, "I am the Way," because he not only shows us how we are to face the difficulties of life, but because he actually enables us, strengthens and upholds us as we face them. So, without knowing what the future holds, we can say that we know the Way, because we have him who is the Way, the Truth, and the Life.

All of us face the uncertainty of what tomorrow may bring. Such a reality could be frightening and depressing. But Jesus Christ, living within us by his Spirit, will never fail us. There will be grace to help in time of need. We don't even have to anxiously worry about what the morrow will bring, because when it gets here, he will be with us, and he will be the Way through it. That's all we need.

Forgive Our Foolish Ways   DECEMBER 8

Genesis 9:8-17 and Mark 1:9-15

*Jesus came to Galilee, preaching the gospel of God, and saying,
"The time is fulfilled, and the kingdom of God is at hand;
repent, and believe in the gospel."* MARK 1:14B, 15

Jesus' baptism marks the beginning of his earthly ministry. He then comes onto the public scene with the message: "The kingdom of God is at hand; repent, and believe in the gospel."

Because God loves us, and because his best can only come as we get rid of the things that stand in the way of receiving his best, we have to be called to repentance over and over again. It is never just a call to change by our own effort. We are never required to climb the steps of heaven in our own strength. The call to repent is always joined with the call to "believe the gospel [the Good News]." In other words, it is always possible to repent, because whatever change we need to make is possible by the grace of God, and is for our good.

Repentance means to turn in the other direction. If we have been fearful, it means turning against our fear and choosing to trust. If we have been grouchy, it means turning against our self-centeredness and choosing to be cheerful. And so on. Too many times we think there is no hope of change. We may know that we have negative attitudes, worries, anxieties, a sour outlook on life—and think, "Well, that's just the way it is. I can't do anything about it." But Jesus is saying, "There is hope. You can change. Believe the Good News. God's kingdom is at hand."

When you look out at a winter landscape—whether it is snow-covered or just barren trees, you can sense that before many weeks, flowers will be emerging from their winter's sleep, trees will put forth leaves and blossoms, and spring will be here. You expect that this will happen because you trust the natural processes. In the same way, you can trust and believe that God is at work in you to bring some wonderful changes. Jesus invites us to repent, to turn—from defeat and hopelessness to faith in his Good News. He gave his life to make this possible, and nothing can keep it from happening if we want it to happen with all our heart.

Mercy Upon All   DECEMBER 9

Romans 11:33-36 and Matthew 16:13-20

For God has consigned all men to disobedience, that he may have mercy upon all. O the depth of the riches and wisdom and knowledge of God! ROMANS 11:32,33A

Paul is dealing with a weighty subject in this letter to the Christians in Rome. He is talking about how we have failed as a human race to meet God's holy standards, and how God has used that condition to do something new and wonderful for us. In the seventh chapter of Romans, Paul tells us that he always has a problem, for when he wants to do good, he finds himself sometimes doing the very thing he hates. Can any of us say we have not had the same problem? Which one of us wants to be crabby, unpleasant, unkind, bitter, jealous, fearful or despondent?

Take heart, Paul says! There is a little secret here. We are all in the same boat! No one is righteous in God's sight. We have all fallen short of his glory, so we can relax, for we are not going to succeed at "being good." God has something better in mind. He has stepped into the scene in the person of his Son, our Lord Jesus Christ, who died a sinner's death—in our place. He rose again from the dead, so that we, too, might rise in newness of life—not in some future glorious state only, but right here. He already accepts and loves us, and when we repent, he forgives us and begins the process of change in our hearts.

This the Christian's Good News. It is the hope for the hopeless, strength for the weak, life in the place of deadness and death. *We can change!* Through his grace and power, God is working within us.

No circumstance can jar us away from what God has done for us in Jesus Christ. Life, death, sickness, aging—they simply make the foundation more precious. Paul sees this and cries out, "O the depth of the riches and wisdom and knowledge of God!" Every day we experience his rich mercy anew. Stand on that foundation and rejoice!

Christmas Memories   DECEMBER 10

Isaiah 7:10-16 and Matthew 1:18-25

Christmas, they say, is for the children. Perhaps you've said that yourself, indicating that some of the sparkle went out of it when there were no children around to enjoy its special feeling. But they also tell us that within each one of us a child is still hidden. I believe that's so, because of the feelings and memories that sometimes come—very reminiscent of feelings that I had as a child. Memories of childhood can be pleasant or bittersweet, still containing some pain. At any rate, whether the child be six or sixty—there's no reason not to celebrate and enjoy the real meaning of Christmas.

They also tell us that many people experience severe self-pity or depression at this season. They say that instead of Christmas being a joyful celebration, the memories are often accompanied by bitterness that things are no longer as they were. So it seems good to think about that as we get ready for another Christmas.

God certainly did not send his Son to make us unhappy. Christmas has gathered a lot of things to itself that have little or nothing to do with its real meaning. Many of those things are harmless in themselves, and help to brighten up the "darkest month of the year" with their gaudy brilliance and color. Where we get off track is when we lose the central message and meaning of Christmas, and begin to concentrate on those outer things that may no longer be available to us.

Don't let any unreal expectation or selfish demand keep you from celebrating and enjoying God's Christmas gift to you. He has given you a Savior, one who loves you and is with you every day. What a gift! Enjoy the good memories, but remember, too, that Christmas is for now.

But You, O Bethlehem . . . DECEMBER 11

Micah 5:2-5A and Luke 1:39-55

But you, O Bethlehem Ephrathah, who are little to be among the clans of Judah, from you shall come forth for me one who is to be ruler in Israel. . . . MICAH 5:2

He has put down the mighty from their thrones, and exalted those of low degree (Luke 1:52).

God's ways are not man's ways. Mankind is awed by strength and power, by prominence and worldly glory.

God's ways are not man's ways. He comes in when no one is looking, so to speak. He enters at a low door, takes a "back seat," and carries out his purposes to the confounding and consternation of the worldly wise.

Bethlehem is an example of this. An insignificant little village a few miles from the royal capital—its only claim to fame was that it was "David's Town." Otherwise there was nothing out of the ordinary in it. Who could take seriously that old prophecy hidden away in the scroll of Micah, "But you, O Bethlehem . . . out of you shall come one who is to be leader of Israel. . . ." The wisdom of the world looked in the palaces of Herod or of Caesar for the ruler. But God's eye, which is also on the sparrow, was on the insignificant little place where his Son would be born.

All of this is to speak to us. Most of us consider ourselves quite insignificant as far as the rushing, passing world is concerned. We may wish we were more important, but we know in our hearts that our place is small. No matter! There is something here to encourage us, whoever we might be, however limited we might find our lives and however confined our circumstances. God's ways are not man's ways. He has a purpose for you. He has set his love upon you, and his will toward you is good. He loves to dwell with the truly lowly and humble of heart. So the first thing we must do is to try to get our hearts as humble as we see our circumstances to be. Pride can live even in the most unlikely places!

The next thing is not to allow our vision to be limited by self-pity or anger or jealousy or resentment at our lot. We cannot, we dare not, measure what God may do with some word we say, some act of faith or courage we may display. It may be the very thing that turns another life Godward. And it will take all eternity to measure the significance of one life turned in faith to our heavenly Father.

God's ways are not man's ways.

Believe in the Gospel   DECEMBER 12

Genesis 9:8-17 and Mark 1:9-15

*The time is fulfilled and the kingdom of God is at hand;
repent and believe in the gospel.*   MARK 1:15

For almost 2,000 years people have spoken and written about these words of Jesus. If it is true in some sense that when Jesus spoke these words "the time was fulfilled," how much more is it true now! We Christians believe that the world is headed somewhere. That makes us a people with a forward look, a people of hope. You cannot be a pessimist and be a Christian, ultimately, because Jesus Christ has come.

But there is another word here: "Repent and believe in the gospel." We have often been reminded that the word "repent" has to do with changing our thinking, our attitudes, our way of looking at things, and our way of living. So it is a big and very important word. It is not something we do once for all, a kind of "unpleasant medicine" we swallow, and then get on with living. It is so basic to our situation that it becomes a perpetual word, a perennial call: keep on changing! Why? Because we are not yet fully what we were meant to be.

But do not be discouraged: believe in the gospel. The good news is that God never asks us to do anything without giving us the grace to do it. Even when we do not want to change, or do not see any need to change, he is still faithful, waiting for us to get a little clearer hold on reality. For all of us (no exceptions!) need to repent and change. The good news, the gospel, is that he wants you to become more like him, and is waiting to help you in the process.

Be Merciful   DECEMBER 13

I Corinthians 15:35-38, 42-50 and Luke 6:27-38

Be merciful, even as your Father is merciful.   LUKE 6:36

It's not as easy as it sounds! Being merciful does not come easily for most of us.

If we're honest, we must admit that we cannot change our feelings. We may deny them and repress them, but we cannot make them suddenly become light and beautiful. So the best thing is to own up to the way we feel inside and take our case to the Lord. "Lord, you know how unmerciful I am in my heart. I am grievously hurt and angry at my situation, and I don't feel kindly at all. Yet I know this is wrong. So in my need I cry out to you to change my heart."

Since God knows all about us, the dark and hidden "us" as well as the nice one we like people to see, and since he loves us still with an unfaltering, unchanging love, we can be sure that he will not despise such a prayer for help. And by his grace, we can become "merciful." We can pray for our "enemies" for their success and their joy.

God is gathering a people to himself who want to be like him. He is calling us out of our darkness into his light, out of our old selfish natures into that which he is growing in us. It is a wonderful, hopeful thing to be among those who feel the tug of his Spirit and who want to follow him. He never despises the prayer of the poor in spirit.

John's Message   DECEMBER 14

Philippians 4:4-7 and Luke 3:7-18

The voice of one crying in the wilderness: Prepare the way of the Lord; make his paths straight.   LUKE 3:4

John the Baptist is one of the most interesting characters in the Bible. He appears out of the desert, strangely dressed and with a fiery message that drew the attention even of King Herod and his unlawful wife. He was so much like the prophets of old that people went out of the city to hear him, and for each of them he had a message. That message was not always to their liking. He called them "a brood of vipers," and warned them that they needed to do something about their lives. They needed to repent.

God's word to us often comes in terms we would just as soon not hear. Our conscience pricks us and makes us uncomfortable when we need to look at some action or attitude that is not pleasing to God. So the message comes to us all, young and old alike: "Prepare the way of the Lord; make his paths straight."

One of the things John emphasized to his hearers was that they should not presume that they were good people, that they had good backgrounds, that they were descendants of Abraham. God was not interested in their pedigrees, but their hearts. That's what counts: our inner attitude, for it is from that inner attitude that all our outward actions proceed.

The wonderful thing about life is that we are never too old to hear and respond to this truth. We can change. The old saying that "you can't teach an old dog new tricks" may be true of dogs, but it is not true of God's children. We are never too old to hear John the Baptist's call to "prepare the way of the Lord; make his paths straight."

Only One Master   DECEMBER 15

I Timothy 2:1-8 and Luke 16:1-13

No servant can serve two masters; for either he will hate the one and love the other, or he will be devoted to the one and despise the other. You cannot serve God and mammon. LUKE 16:13

Jesus is talking here about our hearts. Divided loyalty is a disastrous thing. This is what Jesus is concerned with here—our divided loyalty between God and this world—or between God's interest and self-interest. Very bluntly he says, "You cannot serve two masters."

Yet, when we think about our lives, is it not true that all of us have this divided loyalty? When we pray, do we not have to say honestly, "We have left undone those things which we ought to have done, and we have done those things which ought not to have done?" With Paul we may cry out, "The good that I would do, I do not!" For in truth, our hearts are divided and need to be increasingly unified in our single loyalty to one Master.

How can this come about? I know of no instant formula

or prayer that can achieve it. But by being honest about where we are and about the feelings we have, by acknowledging them before God and being sorry for the dividedness within, by asking him repeatedly to draw us to himself more completely, the division can be healed. If we desire to have but one Master, to love him with all our heart, mind, soul and strength—he will walk with us and bring us to our desired goal. We can count on him.

How Much More! DECEMBER 16

Genesis 18:16-33 and Luke 11:1-13

He was praying in a certain place, and when he ceased, one of his disciples said to him, "Lord teach us to pray. . . ." LUKE 11:1

In the Old Testament lesson today, Abraham, that great man of God and pioneer of faith, learned something important about prayer. He learned that God was more willing to answer that he was to ask. First he began by asking that Sodom be spared if fifty righteous persons could be found in it. God agreed. By stages, Abraham found that God was willing to spare the city if only ten righteous persons could be found in it. You could say that God was five times more willing to spare the city than Abraham had the faith to ask in the beginning.

Jesus taught us a great deal about prayer, too. So many people think of prayer as a way of coercing God or cajoling him into doing something he doesn't want to do. But Jesus did not teach us to think of prayer like that. He taught us to think of God as a loving Father who already knows what we need before we ask. It is important to ask, but not because God needs to be informed!

Jesus then adds that if we, being evil, know how to give good gifts to our children, how much more is our heavenly Fatherly willing to give good things to those who ask him.

Jesus also encourages us to keep on praying, even when the answer seems delayed.

How do we learn about prayer? There is only one sure way—by praying. When the disciples asked Jesus to teach them how to pray, he said to them, "Pray in this way," and then he gave them the Model Prayer, which we call the Lord's Prayer.

Most of us know only the tiniest bit about the mystery of prayer. It is a mystery, because through it we link our little lives with the great, omnipotent, creative Power which rules and guides the universe. That's pretty awesome! So, although God remains a mystery we can never fully understand, the mystery is full of love, light and hope. Prayer links our lives to his life.

Remember, when you pray, that you are doing something infinitely significant. You touch infinity. And remember, too, that God is more willing to answer than we are to ask.

Children of God   DECEMBER 17

Romans 8:12-17 and John 3:1-8

When we cry, "Abba, Father!" it is the Spirit himself bearing witness with our spirit that we are children of God.
ROMANS 8:15B, 16

How often do we stop to think, to enjoy the fact that we are God's own children?

The most important thing in our life is our relationship with God. It is more important than our relationship with our family, more important than our education, our looks, our bank account (or lack of one), more important than what other people think about us or how we feel at the moment! And that relationship is locked up, as it were, in the secret compartment of our hearts. Most of us do not talk easily about our relationship with God, but there in the secret place where only he can see it, is our basic, bedrock relationship—the most important one in our whole life!

God made that relationship in the first place. He has sent his Spirit into our hearts, the unseen Guest, the Life hidden within our life. And the Holy Spirit moves inside us, urging us to really know who we are, and to cry, "Abba! Father!" What the Spirit is saying is, "Be at home with God. His love encompasses you and remains with you whether you are thinking about God or not. But you will be much stronger and happier if you talk with your Father and learn to be at home with him."

Paul adds a little further on in that sentence an important little word. We are children, heirs of God and fellow heirs with Christ, provided . . . "That we suffer with him in order that we may also be glorified with him." What does that mean? Everyone suffers, at least to some extent. Paul is saying that if we are going to inherit all that is ours as God's children, we must choose to suffer *with* him. We do not have to suffer alone. We have the assurance that he will not let our necessary suffering go to waste and come to nothing if we keep our eyes on him and remember who we are. We can offer up the suffering that we are called to experience, saying, "Father, I offer this suffering to you, united to the sufferings of my Lord Jesus Christ. Accept it, and use it, even though I find it hard and bitter to bear. Give me grace, dear Father, to bear it as your child." And he will. It is his most sacred and faithful promise.

Mary's Answer   DECEMBER 18

II Samuel 7:8-16 and Luke 1:26-38

And Mary said, "Behold, I am the handmaid of the Lord; let it
be according to Your word." LUKE 1:38

Of all the human responses to the word of God, none
could be more beautiful or pleasing to God than this
simple response of the blessed maid of Nazareth. She little
knew or realized, I am sure, the full significance of the words
which she sang to her kinswoman Elizabeth, when she said,
"Henceforth all generations will call me blessed" (Luke
1:48).

Little wonder that Christian devotion has always made a
special place for her—not only because she was the tender,
caring mother of our Lord, but because her response to God
was an inspiration and example for us all.

Mary's selection to become the mother of the Savior was
first of all God's choice, and her own assent was a part of his
plan. He does not force any of us to do his will, but gives us
many opportunities to say, as Mary said, "Let it be according to Your word."

Who could say that any Christmas is perfectly happy and
without any tinge of sorrow? The bright colors and cheerful
songs can do their part, but they cannot reach the depths of
our need. When the echoes of the songs die and when the
Christmas trees begin to lose their needles, we need something more lasting, more substantial to carry us through. So
did Mary. In her heart she kept saying, "Let it be according
to Your word."

This Christmas is another reminder from our heavenly
Father of how very much he loves you, how precious you are
in his sight. He sent his beloved Son as his Christmas gift to

you and me. Mary did not know what we know when she said this beautiful word. How much more, now, in the light of all he has done for us and all he has given us, should we say to him, "Let it be according to Your word." The God who sent Jesus cannot do us harm: he is worthy of our trust and obedience. Let us give it to him as best we are able, as our gift of thankfulness and praise.

A Kingdom that Cannot Be Shaken

DECEMBER 19

Hebrews 12:18-29 and Luke 13:22-30

Therefore let us be grateful for receiving a kingdom that cannot be shaken, and thus let us offer to God acceptable worship with reverence and awe.... HEBREWS 12:28

There does not seem to be much in the world that is "unshakable."

But our text speaks of the vital importance that we understand that these are testing times, when our own loyalty and faithfulness to what we know is right and good is being tried.

We Christians have "received a kingdom that cannot be shaken." By this the author meant that, no matter what the fads of the moment may be, no matter what turns history may take, God is still God, and his kingdom will stand for ever. We need faith to believe that this is true. Otherwise we will be like leaves blown about by every change of wind. But if we are swayed from the truth, the truth still remains, and God's kingdom will still not be shaken! That is the glory and wonder of what we have been given. It is an eternal kingdom, and if we are his, we can stand steadfast in that, no matter what.

In other times and place, Christians have paid a high price to remain faithful. One reason they could do this was their faith in the truth of this text. If we are in God's kingdom, the passing world cannot hold our hearts. We know that it is a passing world, and we have something better. We have the eternal God as our refuge, and underneath all the trials and difficulties of life are the Everlasting Arms.

The Riches of His Grace　　　　DECEMBER 20

Ephesians 1:3-10 and Mark 6:7-13

In him we have redemption through his blood, the forgiveness of our trespasses, according to the riches of his grace which he lavished upon us.　EPHESIANS 1:7, 8

Some themes never grow old and can never be exhausted by talking about them. Such is the theme of God's grace. Though its meaning is clear and simple, only the experience of it can truly convey what it's all about.

Grace is the unmerited favor of God. It is completely unearned. Paul says that this is a picture of our relationship with God. We are children of grace.

Somewhere deep in our hearts, we know that we must live by grace and die by grace. It is no accident that the grand old hymn of John Newton, "Amazing Grace," climbed to the top of the charts of popular songs a few years ago.

Why? The song is really John Newton's own testimony. He was a sea captain and a slave trader. But troubled by his lack of inner peace, he read the Bible and prayed. "I was delivered from a fear which long had troubled me," he wrote in his life story. "I began to expect to be preserved, not by my own power and holiness, but by the mighty power and promise of God, through faith in an unchangeable Savior."

It is that same unchangeable Savior who holds out his grace to us today. We have not earned it. We do not deserve it, but because of who he is, God chooses to "lavish" his love upon us. It is God's nature to be gracious to the undeserving!

No matter how unworthy we may feel at the moment, we can lay hold on that Amazing Grace. The more we know our own shortcomings and failures, the sweeter it sounds in our hearts.

Blessed Is She Who Believed   DECEMBER 21

Micah 5:2-4 and Luke 1:39-45

Blessed is she who believed that there would be a fulfillment of what was spoken to her from the Lord. LUKE 1:45

In this remarkable story of the Annunciation of the coming birth of God's Messiah, Mary becomes the first believer. Before anyone else knew that the "fullness of time" had come, Mary, the humble maid of Nazareth, was allowed to respond in faith to God's saving action.

In her response to the message, Mary showed that she had prepared herself to believe, even when what was told her went against reason, logic or prior experience.

Where Mary is a wonderful example and model for all of us is in her willingness to believe that God would fulfill what he promised. That's what we need to learn to do, and what we can choose to do. He has promised that you will have to face no tomorrow without his presence and provision. He has bid us to cast our cares on him, because he cares for us. We can believe that; we can build our lives on it.

Mary was not spared her share of suffering. She had to go all the way to the cross with her divine Son. But there was always grace. And surely, as she said, "All generations shall call me blessed." We can add our Amen to that. "Blessed is she who believed that there would be a fulfillment of that which was spoken to her of the Lord." And we will be blessed as we follow her example of faith!

Depth of Mercy   DECEMBER 22

Romans 11:33-36 and Matthew 16:13-20

For God has consigned all men to disobedience, that he may
have mercy upon all. O the depth of the riches and wisdom and
knowledge of God! ROMANS 11:32, 33A

Paul is dealing with a weighty subject in today's Letter to the Romans. He is talking about how we have failed as a human race to meet God's holy standards, and how God has used that very condition to do something wonderful for us.

Speaking as a Jew, Paul had spent his life trying to be good, living up to the Law. In the seventh chapter of Romans, he says that he always has a problem: when he wants to do good, he finds himself sometimes doing the very thing he hates. Can we say that we do not understand what he is talking about? Which one of us wants to be crabby, unpleasant, unkind, bitter, jealous, fearful or anxious? Yet have we not all found ourselves showing the very characteristics we hate in ourselves and others, and wondered what we could ever do about it?

Take heart, Paul says. There is a little secret here; we are all in the same boat. No one is righteous in God's sight. We have all fallen short of his glory. So we can relax, for we are not going to succeed at "being good."

God has something better in mind than our frantic, tiring effort to "be right" and "be good." Looking at our situation, God simply declares that we are all disobedient children—sinners—and that something has to be done. He has stepped into the scene in the person of his Son, our Lord Jesus Christ—sinless man and perfect God. Jesus lived a perfect life—for us. Then he died a sinner's death—in our place. He rose again from the dead, so that we, too, might rise in newness of life—not just in some future glorious state, but right here. We can experience inner change. Through the grace and mercy of God we can become more free, more loving, less fearful, more trusting.

This is the Christian's good news. It is hope for the hopeless. It is strength for the weak. It is life in the place of deadness and death. God is at work in us. It is not even something we have to do ourselves. It is important to begin to see the truth about who we are apart from him, to want to be changed, and to pray for it. But he does the changing. It is his work, not ours. "It is God who works in you for his good pleasure."

God knew just what we needed, and provided it in Jesus Christ. Every day we experience that mercy in new ways.

Light Within   DECEMBER 23

II Corinthians 4:3-6 and Mark 9:2-9

For it is God . . . who has shone in our hearts to give the light
of the knowledge of the glory of God in the face of Christ.
II CORINTHIANS 4:6

Paul says that we have the "light of the knowledge of the glory of God" in our hearts, shining in the face of Christ. What does this mean to you? Here are some thoughts for your meditation:

Jesus walked in his Father's presence, and even when he was here on earth physically, his disciples were allowed this glimpse of his glory shining through. Today's Gospel tells of the Transfiguration, when Jesus' whole body and even his clothes were transformed into a spiritual radiance. Wherever Jesus went, people were aware of God. When a woman came up in a crowd and touched the hem of his garment, strength and healing flowed to her. People heard him speak, and their response was, "No one ever spoke like this man!"

God's glory is shown forth in divine weakness as Jesus goes to the cross. This remains a mystery to the human mind, but are we not irresistibly drawn to the God who so loved the world that he gave his only Son for us? Here is a glory that needs no glitter, no pomp, no ceremony. It is the glory of selfless, self-giving love—love unto death.

God's glory is shown forth in Jesus' victory over death. This is what the Transfiguration pre-figured. And what it means, as the glory penetrates the darkness and fear of our hearts, is that his victory is ours. Fear lives off the unknown. We dread what we do not know and what we think might happen. But then the light, the glory of God, penetrates that gloom and bids us believe. Like the sunshine coming through the window of our bedroom, it foretells the coming of Day. We are children of the Day, called and redeemed to live in his marvelous light. So we can put away the darkness of dread and anxiety and choose to let his glory lighten our hearts. When doubt comes, look to Jesus. When fear threatens, look to Jesus.

Choose Life   DECEMBER 24

Deuteronomy 30:15-20 and Luke 14:25-33

I have set before you life and death, blessing and curse; therefore choose life, that you and your descendants may live, loving the Lord your God, obeying his voice and cleaving to him.
DEUTERONOMY 30:19B AND 20A

God's plan for Israel was a very simple one. They had languished long in slavery under their Egyptian taskmasters. Now they were to be a free people. They would not even have a king as such. The land before them is described as "flowing with milk and honey." It would be theirs, and they would live in it long and happily under one condition: they were to obey God and his commandments.

If they chose not to obey, rebellion was always a possibility. There were plenty of other nations already showing how to do it! And their own human natures would be ready to help them rebel at any time. There is something in us all that seems to prefer rebellion to obedience. In fact, the sad history shows that they had hardly gotten into the country when they began to ignore God's commandments and worship heathen gods that were already being served by the Canaanite nations. God had warned that to disobey was to bring cursing. They could not choose the consequences of their disobedience.

Today, we have the same choices set before us: life and death. They don't usually come so dramatically labeled, and we may not even be aware that we are choosing them, but they are there all right. We can choose to live totally for ourselves, thinking and caring for no one else, wrapped up in our own little universes, smothered by our self-concern to a sickening degree. Many do, and it is especially tempting to do so when life keeps us from doing the things we have always loved to do or limits the scope of activities we enjoy. I am thinking of times when we may be shut in or confined for a time in a hospital or at home—or living alone, with few opportunities to be with other people. Self-concern can become literally self-consuming!

Yes, the choices are still with us—obedience or rebellion. And so are the consequences.

Moses' urgent plea to the people he loved was, "Choose life!" As you face the little decisions that make up your day, let those words echo in your heart: Choose life. Choose the things that bring more abundant life to you and to those you love. Choose faith. Choose hope. Choose to put down bitterness, jealousy and despair. Choose to pray about your problems instead of pining about them. Whatever things are just, pure, lovely gracious—think about these things! Fill your mind with thoughts of God and lift your eyes to the hills. Choose life. That is what our Lord Jesus Christ came to make possible: life in all its abundance. And it is for you.

O Come, Let Us Adore Him — DECEMBER 25

Luke 2:8-20 and Jeremiah 29:10-14

Let us go over to Bethlehem and see this thing that has happened, which the Lord has made known to us. LUKE 2:15B

At Christmas we think of warm times with friends and family, exchanging gifts and brightening one another's lives. It is always good to remember that "it is more blessed to give than to receive," and that is never more true than at Christmas. So if we want glad hearts, we should look to ways in which we can give to others.

But our text today points in a little different direction. We don't know what kind of gifts the shepherds took to the Bethlehem stable. But we do know that the intent of their heart was not only to see, but to worship. Luke tells us that when they returned to their flocks, they went "praising God for all they had heard and seen, as it had been told them" (Luke 2:20).

The Christmas miracle is almost too great to believe. God chose to enter our human race as a little baby, fully God and fully human. As a human baby, he had his mother Mary to care for him. As the Son of God, he worked miracles that still astound believers and unbelievers alike. His work on earth began in a stable—and it ended on a cross. So Christmas is no "child's game." It is a call to wonder, and to adore the One who has come to rescue us from our sin-cursed world.

How can we adore him? Each one of us must find the answer to that question. Part of the answer is to make time for worship. The shepherds left their flocks and went to Bethlehem. They put their desire to find "the Savior who is Christ the Lord" ahead of their concern for their sheep. If we want to find him in a new and deeper way, we must in our hearts take time to seek him and find him. "You shall seek me and find me," he says in Jeremiah 29:13, "when you seek me with all your heart." We have his assurance that he is to be found, and who does not daily need the fulfillment of that gracious promise?

So let us "go over to Bethlehem" and join the throngs in heaven and on earth who adore him, Christ the Lord!

What Is Your Kingdom? DECEMBER 26

Psalm 119:33-48 and Mark 12:28-34

When Jesus saw that he answered wisely, he said to him, "You are not far from the kingdom of God." MARK 12:34A

Did the scribe go the whole way and enter the kingdom of God? Did he decide that he would become a follower of Jesus? We do not know. But one thing is sure: dealing wisely with the questions of life brings a person near the kingdom of God.

And what is that kingdom? Jesus taught us to pray "Thy kingdom come on earth as it is in heaven." So we know that where God is king, there his kingdom exists. Where his will is done, there his kingdom exists.

There is another "kingdom" at work in the world and in our own lives. The world's spirit is a spirit of "everything for me." That kingdom is in every one of us, making us selfish, jealous, crabby, stubborn and ill-natured when we let it reign in us. On the other hand, when we, like the scribe in today's text, deal wisely with the questions of life, another Spirit takes charge. St. Paul says that the fruit of the Spirit (the Holy Spirit) is "love, joy, peace, long-suffering, gentleness, goodness, faith, meekness and temperance" (Galatians 5:22, 23). Quite an abundant harvest!

For my part, I find it difficult sometimes to deal wisely with the question, "What is important now?" My old self can very quickly assert itself and make its case. But when I allow the Spirit of God to take charge, I find I can say "No" to the demands of my pride, my self-righteousness, even of my anger or hurt—and then peace follows. I think that is a small taste of the kingdom of God.

Temples of God   DECEMBER 27

Exodus 20:1-17 and John 2:13-22

But he spoke of the temple of his body.   JOHN 2:21

Those who were questioning Jesus in today's Gospel were confused and confounded by his use of the word "temple." They naturally assumed that he was speaking of the great Temple of Herod. It was the pride of the nation and the center of religious life. When Jesus said, "Destroy this temple and I will raise it up in three days," the reaction of those who heard Jesus speak these words was so violent that one of the witnesses at Jesus' trial later testified that he heard him say, "I will destroy this temple and raise it up in three days."

But we know that "he spoke of the temple of his body."

What function did the great Temple fulfill in the lives of the people, and why was it so important? First—the temple was the House of God. It was the place where his Name and his honor resided. When Jesus called his body a temple, he was saying that God dwelt within in an intimate and special way. And what was true of him is now true of every one of us who believes in him. God lives within us by his Holy Spirit! We are temples or houses of God.

Second, a temple was a place of sacrifice. Its primary worship was to offer to God the sacrifices of repentance and thanksgiving.

But as temples, we are still to be a place of sacrifice. What kind of sacrifice goes on in these temples of ours? It could be the sacrifice (or offering up) of our pride, our self-righteousness, our strong opinions that separate and divide us from others, our stubborn self-will, and so on. On the altar of our hearts we are to make continual sacrifices of thanksgiving because of the great blessings God has poured out upon us.

Finally, a temple was a place of prayer. Jesus said, "It is written, my house shall be a place of prayer for all people." Is your temple a house of prayer? Do you offer daily prayers—or more frequent ones—to God who is present within you? Do you carry on simple, straightforward conversation with him? That is much better than talking to yourself!

Who Am I? DECEMBER 28

Exodus 3:1-15 and Luke 13:1-9

Who am I that I should go to Pharaoh, and bring the sons of Israel out of Egypt? EXODUS 3:11

When God spoke to Moses on the mountaintop, and appointed him as his chosen instrument for the deliverance of the children of Israel, Moses responded in a way which at first sight seems quite understandable. "Who am I that I should go to Pharaoh?" he asked.

Moses knew all too well who he was, and that is what made him ask the question of God.

With a few changes in wording, I suppose any of us could be describing ourselves.

The interesting thing is that God did not try to change Moses' mind about himself.

God knew that just feeling good about himself would hardly do Moses any good when he stood face to face with the king of all Egypt. Nor does just feeling good about ourselves hold us in good stead when we stand up against the trials and difficulties which we encounter.

What did God do to answer Moses' question about himself? To paraphrase, it was as if God said, "Moses, I know your weaknesses and limitations, but the important thing in this case is not who you are, but who I am. I AM WHO I AM." Only the strength and constancy of Almighty God is unchangeable, able to stand up against the most threatening of forces or circumstances which may come against us.

In the face of difficulty, even of seeming impossibility, we must move the focus of our attention from ourselves to God. He is the great I AM. From his point of view, like the point of view of the vinedresser in our parable from Luke, he sees hope for the weakest of his servants. Nothing, and no one, is useless in his hands. "Who am I?" we ask him. He answers, "You are what you are . . . because I AM."

Cast Down, but Not Destroyed   DECEMBER 29

II Corinthians 4:6-11 and Mark 2:23-3:6

We are afflicted in every way, but not crushed; perplexed but not driven to despair; persecuted, but not forsaken; cast down, but not destroyed. . . . II CORINTHIANS 4:8, 9

If anyone was ever entitled to self-pity, the Apostle Paul certainly was. In this letter to the Christians of Corinth, he catalogued some of the things that had happened to him— and it's a pretty impressive list!

There is an old spiritual which says, "Sometimes I feel discouraged and think it's all in vain." I suspect all of us have had moments like that.

But the old spiritual doesn't stop there. It says, "Sometimes I feel discouraged and think it's all in vain, but then the Holy Spirit revives my soul again!"

What can keep us from being in despair, crushed, destroyed by the circumstances of our lives? Paul says that he was always carrying in his body "the death of Jesus" (II Corinthians 4:10). That sounds strange at first, but he is saying something that can be of real help to us. When Jesus came and joined his life to ours, he took us into himself. We are united with him in his human life and in his death. The death he died was for us, and, in a real sense, we died for him. So if we "carry" the death of Jesus with us we have the seed of victory with us, no matter what comes against us. These things lose their power to defeat us, because Jesus Christ has given us his life. When he rose again and sent the Holy Spirit into our hearts, he gave us inner power to meet every hard place in life without being destroyed by it.

As long as he dwells in us and we in him, we have the inner resources to meet whatever life brings. The power is

not ours, because we are weak, easily frightened, easily overcome. But we have the power—his power—in us, and it is
continually given to us as we need it.

Life may cast us down, but, thanks be to God, it cannot
destroy us!

Inner Healing   DECEMBER 30

Psalm 147 and Mark 1:29-39

*And he healed many who were sick with various diseases, and
cast out many demons; and he would not permit the demons to
speak, because they knew him.*   MARK 1:34

In Jesus' day, there were no hospitals, physicians were few
in number, and medicines were of very limited value. So we
can understand the eagerness with which people crowded to
him as word of his divine power spread throughout Galilee.

There is another aspect of his healing here that is important to us. Jesus is dealing with the disturbances within the
person's mind and heart. He performed his healing also with
his teaching, by which he sought to change attitudes, knowing that attitudes could lead either to health and wholeness
or to sickness and brokenness.

Medical science has awakened to the fine, delicate relationship between emotional health and physical health. A
whole category of ailments (real ones) are termed psychoso-
matic. Simply treating such ailments with medicine does not
cure them. Their roots are deep within the soul.

Think of how Jesus brings inner healing to us today.
First, he teaches us to face honestly who we are, the things
that are wrong with us, the way we have hurt other people,
the places where we have been hurt and need to forgive. We

do that by confessing our wrongness in holding on to these things, asking forgiveness, accepting forgiveness, forgiving ourselves, and then forgiving others. In this wonderful trans- action, the Great Physician, the Divine Forgiver, begins to work life and health within our souls.

Then Jesus bids us trust our heavenly Father. Too many of us worry and fret, trying to take care of ourselves, and take pride in our self-sufficiency. Then we find that in spite of everything, there are circumstances we can't change. But God knows our needs and he cares. God really cares for us. There is life and healing in those words, for they are reality and truth.

Finally, Jesus reminds us that we all need healing within. "I did not come to call the righteous," he said, "but sinners." So that is all of us—no exceptions. Relax. Receive the liber- ating truth: you can find greater healing within than you ever thought possible.

The Day of Small Beginnings DECEMBER 31

Isaiah 61:10-62:3 and Luke 2:22-40

For mine eyes have seen thy salvation, which thou hast prepared before the face of all peoples. LUKE 2:30, 31

Our text is a good word for us to think about in connec- tion with Christmas and the New Year. Simeon was given the insight to see what God was doing in the birth of Jesus. God was preparing his salvation for all peoples, and Simeon had been allowed to know that God would show him the Messiah before he died. So it does not matter to Simeon that there is no fanfare of trumpets, no royal pro- cession, no marching armies to show that God's deliverance has arrived. In his heart he understands that, in this small beginning, God is doing a deed which will be a light to the nations and the glory of Israel.

God does not always do his work in spectacular ways. His greatest work is the change which he makes in our souls—turning us from the darkness of our way, to love him, to trust him, and to hope in him. This is truly a miraculous thing, because we are by nature self-centered. So God undertakes to do a profound thing—to change us into the likeness of his nature. And this is where the "Day of Small Beginnings" is so significant. God works in the hidden depths of our hearts, sometimes slowly, not even observed or noticed by those around us.

For you and for me, the small steps of faith we have already taken are not to be despised. "He who began a good work in you will perform it until the day of Jesus Christ." Hold on to what he has done in you, and expect more. And have a blessed New Year growing in him!